Marketing MCQS

Maxwell Joseph Ranasinghe

Copyright@ Maxwell Joseph Ranasinghe, 2018
Published with arrangement of Kindle Direct Publishing Program
Moral right of the author has been asserted

All rights reserved. Without limiting the rights under copyright reserved above, no part of this publication may be reproduced, stored or introduced into a retrieval system, or transmitted, in any form or by any means (electronic, mechanical, photocopying, recording or otherwise), without the prior written permission of the both the copyright owner and the publisher of this book.

This book is dedicated to my Marketing guru

Late Professor David Morris Jnr.
University of New Haven, Connecticut, USA

Preface

Multiple Choice Questions (MCQs) are used as an objective assessment in almost all the mid-term and final exams of marketing in universities and professional institutions all over the world. The MCQs in marketing are set from the whole syllabus. MCQs generally test the knowledge of fundamental concepts, terms and the ability of students in application of such knowledge in interpreting practical situations. MCQs are tricky and cleverly designed to distract students to mark incorrect answers. The time given to answer MCQs are limited and students should have a thorough knowledge of the subject to select the correct answer within the restricted time. The challenge for students is, they are required to study many subjects in addition to marketing in one semester. Therefore, not every student has the time to go through the whole syllabus and remember all the concepts.

As an experienced lecturer and an examiner in marketing for more than 20 plus years in several universities and professional institutions, I offer students a short cut to learn the fundamental concepts, the way they are tested and how to give correct answers. Hence, this book will take away a big burden on students in reading the whole syllabus, sifting, selecting important concepts, terms and memorizing all of the them. This book contains most of the frequently asked questions, so that a student could easily study for the MCQ exam. In addition to helping students in answering MCQs, this book provides a revision of the whole syllabus offered in a marketing course. Therefore, the knowledge gathered by answering MCQs in this book will surely help the student to write short and essay type answers as well with confidence.

This book is periodically updated by going through the questions asked in exams, interviewing students and taking into account the developments in the subject of marketing.

MCQs on Information and Communication Technology for Marketing are included in this book as it has become a new area of testing in marketing MCQs.

I thank all the students who buy this book and do hope it will help greatly in passing your exams with excellent grading.

My best wishes
Maxwell Ranasinghe

Table of Contents

Preface

Chapter 1: Introduction to Marketing

Chapter 2: Marketing Environment

Chapter 3: Marketing Mix

Chapter 4: Marketing Research

Chapter 5: Consumer Behavior

Chapter 6: Segmenting, Targeting and Positioning

Chapter 7: Product

Chapter 8: Price

Chapter 9: Promotion

Chapter 10: Distribution

Chapter 11: Marketing Planning

Chapter 12: Information Communication Technology for Marketing

Chapter 1
MCQs on Introduction to Marketing

1. **Marketing has its origins in**
    1. Economics
    2. Philosophy
    3. Mathematics
    4. Sociology

2. **Marketing attempts to satisfy needs and wants by**

    1. Advertising

    2. Supplying goods and services

    3. Developing products

    4. Improving quality of goods and services

3. **Utility is a concept of economics that has four basic kinds. Namely,**

    1. Demand, supply, market, consumers

    2. Electricity, water, air and gas

    3. Form, time, place and possession

    4. Money, machines, men and means

4. **Marketing should be an organizational function that creates value to,**

    1. Customers

    2. Suppliers and shareholders

    3. Society and environment

    4. All of the above

5. **Because of international economic agreements, growth of information technology and commonly acceptable currencies,**

    1. Multinationals have dominated all the trade in the

world

2. Markets have expanded beyond national boundaries

3. Consumers are able to buy goods at lower prices

4. Manufacturing has become complex

6. Sellers' market is where,

1. More sellers sell their products in the market

2. Sellers are competing on price and quality with each other

3. Sellers are in one single geographic location offering goods to the customers coming to the market

4. More buyers exists for fewer goods and services

7. Buyer's market is where,

1. Buyer stays in one geographical location and the sellers visit them to sell their products

2. More goods and services are offered by sellers than what is wanted by buyers

3. Buyers are more quality conscious

4. Buyers show great interest in buying goods

8. The concept that goods can be sold easily, if you produce goods at a lower cost and make it available, is advocated by,

1. Product Concept

2. Production Concept

3. Sales Concept

    4. Marketing Concept

9. Sales concept advocates that,
    1. Sellers should offer best prices to win sales
    2. Salesmen should understand the customer needs well
    3. Consumers have a lethargic attitude in buying goods and services and they have to be persuaded to buy good by advertising and promoting
    4. Sales is the most important part of marketing

10. What is the concept that focuses more about finding needs of the consumer before you produce goods?
    1. Marketing Concept
    2. Production Concept
    3. Sales Concept
    4. Product Concept

11. What is the concept that focuses more about the quality and features about the product?
    1. Marketing Concept
    2. Production Concept
    3. Sales Concept
    4. Product Concept

12. Expanded notion of Relationship Marketing describes about,
    1. Having a long-term relationship with customers to

develop sales

2. Developing a long-term relationship with marketing channels of distribution

3. Cost effective relationship with customers, suppliers, employees and other stakeholders for mutual benefit

4. Importance of developing a relationship with competitors to control the market place

13. When a company is only product oriented and not consumer oriented, it could be called as,

1. Product specialist marketing
2. Marketing myopic
3. Wider scope marketing
4. Lean marketing

14. When a politician conducts a campaign for his candidature for election,

1. It could be called as person marketing
2. It could be called as election marketing
3. It could be called as political services marketing
4. It could be called as political party marketing

15. Place Marketing is,

1. Advertising of distribution points

2. Allocating geographical areas to different salespersons

3. Placing products in a place where customers can see it very well

4. Effort to attract customers to a particular geographical location

16. When a religious organization puts up posters and banners about its annual events or religious ceremonies among the public,

1. It is not called marketing
2. It is called religious marketing
3. It is called not-for-profit marketing
4. It is called social marketing

17. When a company markets its products to another company,

1. It is called marketing to manufacturers of goods and services
2. It is called Business to Business marketing
3. It does not use mass media marketing
4. It sends a senior marketing person to talk to the other company

18. When an NGO launches a campaign to discourage using phone whilst driving,

1. It is conducting negative marketing

2. It is engaged in the work that a government should do
3. It is going out of their mandate
4. It is doing cause marketing

19. Social Marketing is,
1. Marketing products to poor communities of the society
2. Marketing products to the social services organizations
3. Using online social media such as Facebook to communicate marketing messages
4. Making marketing facilities available for the poor people to sell their products

20. Buzz Marketing is,
1. Using loyal customers of a company to spread a positive experience of the products and services of a company
2. Installing a buzzer for the customers in a restaurant to call waiting staff as and when needed
3. Using busses to carry advertising messages of the company
4. Asking customers to talk about negative experiences when dealing with competitors

21. Two major categories of Traditional Marketing were.

    1. People and goods

    2. Goods and services

    3. Person and events

    4. International and national

22. Traditional marketing has evolved and broadened its scope to include,

    1. Marketing of persons, places, causes, events ideas and organizations

    2. Marketing of fixed phones to mobile phones

    3. Marketing of websites

    4. Marketing of technology

23. Example of an event marketing is,

    1. Marketing an eventful life story of a celebrity

    2. Managing an event

    3. Marketing a sporting, musical or cultural activity to a selected a target market

    4. Marketing videos of a musical event

24. An attempt to influence a person to help a public library by accepting its objectives and goals is called,

    1. Organizational marketing

    2. Cause marketing

    3. Social Marketing

4. Service marketing

25. Continued customer service during and after sales is advocated by the notion of,
   1. Transaction based marketing
   2. Virtual marketing
   3. Buzz marketing
   4. Relationship marketing

26. Mobile marketing is,
   1. Sending commercial messages through wireless technology
   2. Advertising by mobile vehicles
   3. People going around streets displaying advertising boards
   4. Marketing messages of mobile phone distributors

27. A Vehicle parts distributor partners with a parts installation workshop to provide services to its customers at a discounted price. This is an example for,
   1. Syndicate marketing
   2. Strategic alliance
   3. Customer benefit program
   4. Profit sharing program

28. A product in demand by customers is produced by a

company, but the company is aware that it could be potentially harmful to consumers in the long term. What statement matches with this?

1. It is a legal issue
2. It is an ethical issue
3. Company need not worry as it is demanded by customers and choice is given for the customers to choose
4. The company has no responsibility as it is only potentially harmful and it is not proven

29. The notion of making profits as the main responsibility has now changed. A marketer should now care about,

1. Employees, customers and society
2. Respect human rights
3. Protect the environment
4. All of the above

30. Sustainable marketing is,

1. Saving money from the profits to use in difficult times to sustain the business
2. Producing goods and services that are only essential to sustain life of customers
3. Producing products with least impact on the human and natural environment
4. Supporting employees to practice sustainable

consumption methods in their homes

31. Marketing covers the activities of non- business entities. Which one suits this description?

    1. IBM selling computers to a non-government organization

    2. Unilever conducting free program on hygiene

    3. A Church/ Temple/ Mosque/Kovil putting up banners around the town about a religious festival

    4. Non-governmental organization filing action against a mining company for pollution

32. What statement describes marketing in a better way?

    1. We must produce what we can from the resources and skills we have

    2. We need to vigorously persuade customers to buy our products

    3. We need to understand customer needs first before making products

    4. We should produce best quality products

33. If a company is selling fast food like McDonalds,

    1. They should offer a variety of products

    2. They should have affordable prices

    3. They should establish outlets at convenient places for customers

4. All of the above

34. Which one of the statements below is not a task of marketing?

    1. Analyzing markets

    2. Setting prices

    3. Learning about the changes in the economy

    4. Building a factory for produce products for market

35. Occasionally torrential rains force families to leave their homes and loose their household equipment due to floods. For an insurance company, what is this?

    1. Area to avoid business

    2. Opportunity to enter into new business

    3. Propose government to develop a fund

    4. Propose an NGO to come into rescue

36. Religious institutions proposes the government to close all the places that sell alcoholic beverages within a 5km radius of places of worship and schools. This move for a distillery is a,

    1. Marketing environment factor

    2. Marketing mix factor

    3. Consumer behavior issue

    4. Relationship factor with religious institutions

37. A big fund owned by a religious organization withdraws its

investment on fossil fuel companies. This can be seen as,

    1. Responding to social and ethical needs

    2. Adhering to laws of the country

    3. Avoiding investment risk as solar power is becoming more popular

    4. Managing a diversified portfolio of investments

38. A company uses Nano-technology and produces a clothing material that will not gather dirt and sweat. What should the company do first to establish the market?

    1. Promote the benefits and create awareness among its customers

    2. Have a premium price

    3. Let its' distributors know about the invention

    4. Produce all their clothing by using the new material

39. Starting point of marketing is the target market and focus is on needs of the customers. However, in sales, the starting point and focus is on

    1. Factory and product

    2. Promotion and sales volume

    3. Revenue and profits

    4. Sales coordination and Distribution

40. Iceberg Theory says

    1. 1/10 of marketing is not visible

2. 9/10 of marketing is not visible

3. 1/10 of customers know what is marketing

4. 9/10 of customers buy only tangible products

41. A group of connected goods and services across diverse set of industries is called as,

1. Market place

2. Meta market

3. Market space

4. Resource Market

42. The internet has created an electronic information exchange environment in which the constraints of physical boundaries are eliminated. It has integrated multitude of market places through technology. This new phenomenon is called,

1. World Market

2. Market Space

3. Mega Market

4. Meta Market

43. Latent demand means,

1. When a consumer shares a strong need that cannot be satisfied by an existing product

2. Product demanded after purchasing a product

3. Drop in the demand for goods

4. Demand for goods during the period of lent

44. The societal marketing concepts holds that the organization's task is to determine the needs, wants, and interests of target markets and to deliver the desired satisfactions more effectively and efficiently than competitors in a way that ………………….the consumer's and the society's well-being.

    1. Develops

    2. Manages

    3. Preserves or enhances

    4. Expands

45. Long term success of business mainly depend on providing……………….

    1. Customer needs at a lower price

    2. Customer value

    3. High quality products

    4. Environment friendly products

46. Marketing is usually perceived by the public as,

    1. Introduction of new product concepts and improvements.

    2. Advertising and promotion activities.

    3. A process of satisfying customer needs.

4. System of exploiting customers

47. A simulation of the real marketplace where buyers and sellers could be connected to negotiate transactions is called,

1. Model Market

2. Artificial Market

3. Virtual Market

4. Quasi Market

48. A marketing philosophy summarized by the phrase "a good quality product will sell itself" is a characteristic of the………….. era.

1. Production

2. Product

3. Marketing

4. Relationship

49. Which of the following factors contributed to the transition from the production period

  to the sales period?

1. Increased consumer demand

2. Increased capacity of production and competition among

the suppliers

    3. Increase in customer income

    4. Deregulation of markets

50. One of the major aims of customer relationship management is to increase………

    1. Short terms sales

    2. Customer loyalty and equity

    3. Company image

    4. The product range

51. Local marketing is also called as,

    1. Location based marketing

    2. Neighborhood marketing

    3. Selling local products

    4. Both 1 and 2 are correct

52. In order for transaction in marketing to be completed, the following should take place,

    1. There should at least be two parties

    2. Each party has something that might be of value to the other party

    3. Each party is capable of communication and delivery

    4. All of the above

53. Marketing is considered as a,

    1. Business philosophy

    2. Business function

    3. Business philosophy as well as a business function

    4. Division that makes sales

54. "MAAD" Mothers Against Drunk Driving are advocating to discourage people driving under the influence of alcohol. This is called marketing of,

    1. A Great need of the society

    2. An idea

    3. An important issue

    4. Service

55. If a company like McDonalds introduces a burger with low calories in response to consumer demand, it is following the,

    1. Selling concept

    2. Marketing concept

    3. Production concept

    4. Product concept

56. If companies like Tesla introduces a car totally driven by battery and solar power, they are complying with,

    1. Production concept

    2. Green marketing concept

    3. Marketing concept

    4. Product concept

57. A stronger focus on social and ethical concerns in marketing is advocated by,

    1. Marketing Concept

    2. Social marketing

    3. Societal Marketing Concept

    4. Green Marketing Concept

58. If a company, in addition to its typical marketing activities, is trying to manage other elements of a firm's external environment such as government, media, and pressure groups, it is called,

    1. Lobbying

    2. Market power

    3. Mega- marketing

    4. Dominance

59. Heart share and Mind Share are terms used in,

   1. Psychological Segmentation

   2. Advertising and Promotion

   3. Consumer behavior

   4. Analysis of demand

60. Mind share relates generally to the development of consumer ………………….. Heart share –relates generally to the preferences based on …………………

   1. Awareness – Emotions

   2. Attitude – Response

   3. Credibility – Prejudice

   4. Loyalty – Family

Chapter 1
MCQs on Introduction to Marketing Answers Key

1. 1
2. 2
3. 3
4. 4
5. 2
6. 4
7. 2
8. 2
9. 3
10. 1
11. 4
12. 3

13. 2
14. 1
15. 4
16. 3
17. 2
18. 4
19. 3
20. 1
21. 2
22. 1
23. 3
24. 1
25. 4
26. 1
27. 2
28. 2
29. 4
30. 3
31. 3
32. 3
33. 4
34. 4
35. 2
36. 1
37. 1
38. 1
39. 1
40. 2
41. 2
42. 2
43. 1
44. 3
45. 2
46. 2
47. 3
48. 2
49. 2
50. 2
51. 4
52. 4
53. 3
54. 2

55. 2
56. 2
57. 3
58. 3
59. 2
60. 1

Chapter 2
MCQs on Marketing Environment

1. The three main components of the marketing environment are,

    1. Organizational Environment, Operational (Task) Environment and Macro Environment

    2. Internal Environment, Ecological Environment and Market Environment

    3. Human Environment, Natural Environment and Artificial Environment

    4. Corporate Environment, Political Environment and Technological Environment

2. External elements of the marketing environment are,

    1. Staff Relationships, Resource Constraints and Corporate Culture

    2. Competitors, Suppliers, Consumers and The Publics

    3. Political, Economic, Sociological, Technological

and Environmental and Legal

4. Markets, Customers, Suppliers and Regulators

3. Which statement is true?

1. Formal organizational structure cannot be shown in a chart
2. Informal organizational structure can be shown in a chart
3. Both above points 1 and 2 are wrong
4. Both above points 1 and 2 are correct

4. Suppliers and customers are in the firm's,

1. Economic environment
2. Social environment
3. Task/ intermediate environment
4. Psychological environment

5. Which of the following environment is affected by change in the values and belief systems?

1. Psychological environment.
2. Cultural environment.
3. Internal environment.
4. Demographic environment.

6. Why do marketers study marketing environment?
   1. Mainly to try to achieve organizational objectives by predicting and influencing it
   2. Since environment must be protected
   3. Since it is a major part of the marketing planning
   4. To please the employees, customers and regulators

7. Identify the best answer for a strategic alliance:
   1. Computer manufacturing company join hands with food distribution company
   2. Food manufacturing company join hands with food distribution company
   3. Mobile phone manufacturer join hands with banking corporation
   4. Car manufacturing company combines resources with a jet manufacturing company

8. A local toy manufacturers association meets government officers to influence them to increase taxes on importation of toys. This is called,

   1. Lobbying
   2. Requesting sympathy
   3. Requesting to stop dumping foreign products

4. Requesting qualitative controls on imports

9. A strategic alliance of two or more companies in an industry may expect to,

1. Have a competitive advantage over other players
2. Share risk and profits
3. Both above 1 and 2
4. Create disruption in the market place

10. In a free market economy, monopolies are discouraged. However, patent rights allow certain companies like drug manufacturers to get a monopoly for a limited period. Why is this?

1. To protect their brand names
2. To allow companies to the maximize profits
3. To test the market
4. To recoup the millions spent of developing and launching the product

11. The study of competitive strategy helps a firm to determine answers to three questions. These questions are:

1. Should we compete, what market we should compete and how should we compete
2. How tough is the market place, nature of firms in the market place and regulatory aspects

3. The size of the competition, what products they sell, technology they use

4. The management styles of competitors, their capabilities and issues they have

12. When pizza makers compete with hamburgers and sandwiches,

1. It is called direct competition
2. It is called indirect competition
3. Both above 1 and 2
4. None of the above

13. Time based competition is,

1. Strategy of developing and distributing goods and services more quickly than competitors
2. Waiting for the correct time to enter into competition
3. Compete only in the seasons that goods are in demand
4. Making products that are available for only 24 hours

14. Comparatively time-based competition has become a prominent feature in rapidly changing markets of,

1. Mobile phones and computers

2. Seasonal vegetables and fruits
3. Household appliances and furniture
4. Banking and airline services

15. Predatory pricing is illegal under antitrust laws, because it,

1. Sets the price below cost to eliminate competition
2. Sets prices very high where poor consumers may not be able to buy the product
3. Sets the price to be suitable only for major players in the market place
4. Sets the price with hidden charges

16. In developed markets: Price fixing, predatory pricing, bid rigging and misleading advertising are considered as,

1. Civil offences
2. Criminal Offences
3. Moral issues
4. Ethical issues

17. Price fixing is when,

1. All sellers sell at a fixed price
2. Sellers collude among themselves to set prices higher than they would be in a free market
3. Fixing the labels of prices to products in display
4. Showing a higher price on top of the price tag and

fixing a label with a lower price under the old price tag. (locked down price)

18. If a seller tries to attract customers with one or few products offered at lower prices and finally offers higher priced products indicating that the low priced products are not available, this is called,

    1. Predatory pricing

    2. Referral selling

    3. Tied selling

    4. Bait-and switch selling

19. When a seller offers price reductions or other benefits for a customer that provides information about a potential buyer, this is called,

    1. Tied selling

    2. Double ticketing

    3. Referral pricing

    4. Bait-and switch pricing

20. Bid rigging,

    1. Is where competitors collude and agree that only one bid will be made to get the contract of supply

    2. Is where competitors agree in collusion to bid several bids allowing the lowers bidder to get the contract of supply

3. Both above 1 and 2 are correct

4. Only 1 above is correct

21. Hydro electricity supply company is having an issue of meeting the demand. What it should do ethically is to,

    1. Increase the rates

    2. Decrease the rates

    3. Use de-marketing to reduce consumption

    4. Develop Coal power plants to generate electricity

22. What is consumerism?

    1. Consumers buy different types of products without giving much care to its utility value

    2. Consumers follow trends in the markets place and buy products

    3. A social force that aids and protects the buyer by exerting legal, moral pressure on businesses.

    4. The way that consumers behave in a free market

23. These rights have provided the conceptual framework in North America to formulate legislation protecting consumers:

    1. Right to free expression, education and health

    2. Right to choose, be informed, be heard and be safe

    3. Right to vote, become a political candidate and be

elected

4. Right to water, sanitation and housing

24. Phishing, SMiShing and Vishing are terms used to,
    1. Denote new apps in mobile phones to communicate confidentially with friends
    2. Denote new digital marketing terms
    3. Denote digital crimes
    4. Denote extended marketing mix of the e-commerce platforms

25. Dumping is an unethical issue related to,
    1. Distribution
    2. Products
    3. Price
    4. Promotion

26. Bait-and –switch and bribery are unethical issues related to,
    1. Distribution
    2. Product
    3. Promotion
    4. Pricing

27. Deceptive pricing and planned obsolesce of products are unethical issues related to,

1. Pricing and distribution
2. Pricing and product
3. Pricing and promotion
4. None of the above

28. What is the largest civil settlement paid in history (up to 2017) for a product related damages?
1. Tobacco manufacturers paid USD 40 Billion as damages in USA
2. Tobacco manufacturers paid USD 206 Billion in USA
3. Car manufacturer Volkswagen paying USD 14.7 million
4. Agro Chemical company Scott Miracle grow paid USD 12.5 Million

29. The diverse social issues that a marketer faces can be of two categories:
1. Marketing Ethics and Social Responsibility
2. Internal and External
3. Environmental and Technological
4. Political and Social

30. What is the function of the interface between the organization and the society?
1. Production

2. Human Resources

3. Marketing

4. Only marketing research and advertising

31. Marketing ethics is,

1. Marketers standard of conduct and moral values

2. Social and religious values

3. Marketing Institutes of code of conduct for its members

4. Adhering to laws of a specific country or market

32. Widespread use of data bases, analysis of purchase records, selling of address list and consumer information has created,

1. Problems for marketing research

2. An invasion of privacy of consumers

3. Competition among software companies to sell data driven marketing

4. Confusion among marketers about identifying consumer's real needs and wants

33. Corporate Social Responsibility advocates,

1. Making profits to Shareholders

2. Making value to Customers

3. Making value to employees, and care for the wellbeing of the environment and society

4. All of the above

34. The Four dimensions of Archie Carrol's Pyramid of Social Responsibility are:

1. Economic, Legal, Ethical and Philanthropic
2. Economic, Social, Ethical and Democratic
3. Ethical, Social, Charity and Sharing
4. Employment, Profit sharing, Welfare and payment of Taxes

35. If a company is trying to reduce non-biodegradable packaging,

1. It is an innovative company
2. It is adopting green marketing
3. It is adopting state of the art packing
4. it is trying to reduce the cost of packing

36. Which one of the following will reflect negatively on the long term on a company?

1. Periodically let company employees know the ethical issue relating to the company's business
2. Incorporating CSR into core operations of the business
3. Reward employees who develop business in any manner
4. Punish employees who breach the code of ethics of

the company

37. The best salesman of pharmaceutical marketing company reveals that his secret of getting more sales is sponsoring doctor's weekly meetings at a hotel. What should be the onus of the company?

    1. The company should encourage other sales persons also to use that kind of tactics

    2. The company should withdraw the best salesman award from the sales person

    3. Company should discourage other sales person from doing such tactics

    4. Above 2 and 3 should be done if the company is an ethical company

38. All the following relate to Corporate Social Responsibility, but what specifically relates to employees?

    1. Health and safety in the factory

    2. Prevention of water pollution

    3. Developing biodegradable packaging

    4. Supporting a school to develop a mosquito eradication program

39. Marketing efforts are specifically aimed at,

    1. Distributing something at value to buyers and sellers

2. Facilitating satisfying exchange relationships

3. Developing new products for target markets

4. Understanding buyer behavior to meet buyer needs

40. "No Duma" a smokeless cigarette failed in the market because it could not be lit easily with a match. A gas lighter has to be used for few seconds. This failure was due to,

    1. Distribution issue

    2. Products development and testing issue

    3. Poor customer awareness

    4. Poor advice on usage of product

41. An association is advocating not to drink and drive. What are they marketing?

    1. A service

    2. An idea

    3. A public message

    4. A slogan

42. Unilever introduces a low sodium butter in response to customers' demand. The company is following,

    1. Production concept

    2. Product concept

    3. Marketing concept

    4. Selling concept

43. Marketers generally consider that political forces are,

    1. Not important to their activities

    2. Beyond their control

    3. Easy to be influenced

    4. Influenced by international forces

44. Marketing strategy during an economic recession should be,

    1. To reduce the sales force

    2. To reduce advertising and promotion

    3. To offer value and utility

    4. To increase marketing expenditure to win over competitors

45. A trend is --------------------.

    1. Something that has not happened in the past but would happen in future

    2. Unpredictable and short-lived

    3. A direction of events that has happened in the past and that may continue in the near future at least in short term.

    4. A direction or sequence of events that has no momentum and certainty

46. The Managing Director of the company says that they need to minimize environmental damage in all forms of its

activities. What is he advocating?
1. Risk reduction
2. Green Marketing
3. Damage reduction
4. Product Stewardship

47. The marketing manager states that the company needs to sell what is produced by the production department even if it is not the product that is really wanted by the customer. This statement could be named as,

1. Marketing Myopia
2. Selling Unsought Goods
3. Surplus Marketing
4. De- Marketing

48. Unilateral or multilateral agreements between countries are part of the,
1. Macro environment
2. Micro environment
3. International Environment
4. Trade Environment

49. Economic sanctions imposed by countries on other countries are mainly based on,
1. Economic Environment
2. Political Environment

3. Bilateral relations

4. Multilateral relations

50. Motor vehicle manufacturers who were pre- occupied in developing alternative energy driven vehicle are now rolling out vehicles with Automatic Emergency Brake (AEB) or Pre- Collision Systems. This is done,

1. To set new standards of vehicle manufacturing

2. To showcase individual car manufactures technical prowess

3. As a response to mounting social pressure to develop safer vehicles

4. As a response to government regulations on vehicle safety

Chapter 2

MCQs on Marketing Environment

Answers Key
1. 1
2. 3
3. 3
4. 3
5. 2
6. 1
7. 2

8. 1
9. 3
10. 4
11. 1
12. 2
13. 1
14. 1
15. 1
16. 2
17. 2
18. 4
19. 3
20. 4
21. 3
22. 3
23. 2
24. 3
25. 3
26. 3
27. 2
28. 2
29. 1
30. 3
31. 1
32. 2
33. 4
34. 1
35. 2
36. 3
37. 4
38. 1
39. 2
40. 2

41. 2
42. 3
43. 2
44. 3
45. 3
46. 3
47. 1
48. 1
49. 2
50. 3

Chapter 3
MCQs of Marketing Mix

1. Which of the following statements are correct?

    1. Marketing Mix is a set of controllable tactical marketing tools that the firm can blend to produce the response it needs from the market

    2. The marketing mix consists of everything the firm can do to influence the demand for its products

    3. Only above 1 is correct

    4. Both above 1 and 2 are correct

2. Marketing Mix covers,

    1. The strategic decisions that a company takes to sell its products

    2. An analysis of external and internal environmental factors that affects selling of its products

3. A combination of strategic elements available to the marketer to win customers in a given market

4. How product and price be blended to beat the competition and win customers

3. In general, the "P" which is missing in most of the products and services offered by public sector is,
    1. Product
    2. Price
    3. Promotion
    4. Place

4. Most important elements in the marketing mix are,
    1. Product and Price
    2. Place and Promotion
    3. Product, Promotion and Place
    4. Correct blend of above 1 and 2

5. 4 Ps Marketing mix was developed in 1960 by,
    1. McCarthy
    2. Phillip Kotler
    3. Booms and Bitner
    4. Michael Porter

6. The extended marketing mix 7 Ps were developed in 1981 by,
    1. McCarthy

2. Kotler

3. Booms and Bitner

4. Michael Porter

7. Traditionally marketing mix is comprised of 4 P's. They are:

1. People, Place, Product and Price

2. Physical evidence, Promotion, People and Price

3. Product, Price, Place and Promotion

4. Product, Place, Price and Processors

8. The product has its own mix. Major elements of the product mix are,

1. Variety, design, brand name, image, features and benefits

2. Packaging, styling, accessories, warranty, aftersales services

3. Both 1 and 2 are correct

4. None of the above is correct

9. There are many elements that a company must consider in pricing a product. Out of these, what is the most fundamental element?

1. Cost of the product

2. Profit Margin to the wholesalers

3. Profit Margin to the retailers

4. Government Taxes

10. A product will not sell in the market place,

        1. If the product is not attractively packed

        2. If the price is not affordable to the consumers

        3. If the product is not advertised in the television

        4. If the product is sold only online

11. A marketing manager of a company was discussing about importance of inventory control in winning the market share. He is talking about an element that belongs to,

        1. Price

        2. Place

        3. Promotion

        4. Product

12. Fundamental to any promotion campaign is to know,

        1. About the target market well

        2. About the different channels available to advertise

        3. About how major competitors promote their products

        4. Above 2 and 3

13. What does it mean by "AIDA" in marketing?

        1. Awareness, Interest, Decision, Agreement

        2. Action, Intention, Discounts, Advertising

        3. Awareness, Interest, Desire, Action

4. Announcement, Inquiry, Discipline, Attention

14. Key characteristics of an effective marketing Mix are,
    1. Product, Price, Place and Promotion
    2. Physical evidence, Processors and People
    3. Above 1 and 2
    4. Matches customer needs, corporate resources, create competitive advantage and well blended

15. If the marketing mix is to match the customers' acceptance,
    1. The Marketer should understand the customers' needs
    2. The Marketer should understand the behavior of customer in the market place
    3. Both above points 1 and 2 are correct
    4. None of the above is correct

16. Elements of marketing mix are interdependent and a change in one element may affect the total mix. That is why the marketers need to,
    1. Understand the customers well
    2. Blend the marketing mix well
    3. Understand the competition well
    4. Analyze the internal pricing and product strategy well

17. What are the three additional P's that are added to the conventional/ traditional marketing mix?

    1. People, Presentation, Processors

    2. People, Physical evidence, Processors

    3. People, Programs, Promotion

    4. Preparation, Process, Procurement,

18. Why were three additional P's introduced to the 4 P's?

    1. Because services could not be addressed through the traditional marketing mix

    2. Because services differ from physical goods

    3. Both 1 and 2 are correct

    4. None of the above is correct

19. Services differ from physical goods mainly because,

    1. They are variable, intangible, inseparable and perishable

    2. They belong to operations of marketing

    3. They are done by people

    4. They are more difficult than producing a physical good

20. Marketing Manager was discussing the importance of complaint handling. Complaint handling,

    1. Is a part of people and processors in marketing

    2. Is a part of promotion in marketing

3. Is a part of administration in marketing

4. Has nothing to do with marketing

21.. A customer was complaining about the facilities in the waiting area. It belongs to what part of the Marketing mix?

    1. It is part of the processors

    2. It is part of the physical evidence

    3. It is part of the promotion

    4. It is part of the place

22. The environment of the service delivery belongs to,

    1. Processors

    2. Physical evidence

    3. People

    4. Promotion

23. Physical evidence conveys,

    1. The competitiveness of the product or service

    2. The technology associated with the product or service

    3. The coordination of services

    4. Image of the company and its services

24. Four P's Product, Price, Place and Promotion of the marketing mix can be interpreted in the view point of customer in Four C's. The Four C's denote:

1. Consideration, Cost, Convenience and Communication
2. Customer Solution(Value), Cost, Convenience and Commination
3. Confirmation, Cost, Convenience and Connection
4. Customer Expectation, Cost, Coordination and Confirmation

25. Banks have innovated their services to meet the increasing demand of customers for better service. ATMs are installed even at shopping malls. It is part of,
1. Product
2. Place
3. Promotion
4. Physical evidence

26. Which one of the following is not an element in the extended marketing mix?
1. People
2. Place
3. Processors
4. Physical evidence

27. Meeting the demand by customers for safer cars, car manufacturers are now coming out with cars that will not collide with other vehicles in front. (Automatic Emergency Brakes –

(AEB)) This is a part of,

1. Product
2. Brand
3. Strategy
4. Objectives

28. A webinar was organized by a company to talk about its latest service. This is a part of,

1. Promotion
2. Digital marketing
3. e- commerce
4. New channel

29. The government increased the age limit of the customers who can buy alcohol. This has relevance to,

1. Marketing Mix
2. Marketing Ethics
3. Marketing Environment
4. Marketing Concept

30. A company says that they have produced the best product that suits the demand of the customers, has advertised the product and marked it at an affordable price. What is missing in this offering?

1. Pricing

2. Promotion

3. Place

4. Product

31. "Marketing Mix is the most visible part of the marketing strategy of an organization."

    1. True

    2. False

32. What is the basic element of a service which makes it different from a product?

    1. Brand

    2. Package

    3. Price

    4. Intangibility

33. "7 P's in marketing are formed in keeping the offline markets but it includes all the elements that are necessary to cover the online market phenomena as well."

    1. True

    2. False

34. 7 P's of marketing are more,

    1. Internally oriented

    2. Externally oriented

3. Profit oriented

4. Competitor oriented

35. One of the major criticisms of the marketing Mix is that,

1. It does not focus on customer

2. It does not consider competition

3. It does not consider relationships

4. It is not used practically in most of the business

36. In the early stages of the introduction of a product, what would be the status of the element "Product" in the marketing mix?

1. Risk is high

2. Quality problems may occur

3. Product mix may go through few changes

4. All of the above

37. When a product reaches the growth stage, it will face the struggle of retaining distinctiveness. What solution can be proposed?

1. Advertising mix should be changed

2. Price mix should be changed

3. Product mix should be changed

4. Place mix should be changed

38. In the growth stage, many distributors will take part in the

distribution of similar products. What type of approach in place mix would be taken?

    1. Develop good relationships with leading distributors
    2. Make the product available in all distributors and block the competitors distributing the product
    3. Provide better discounts to distributors
    4. Warn distributors from selling similar products

39. In the growth stage of a product, what would be the status of the element "Promotion" in marketing mix?

    1. Promotion cost per unit would be high
    2. Promotion cost per unit would be less
    3. Promotion is not very important
    4. Promotion will be directed at making awareness

40. According to the price/quality strategy model, when a company overprices its
product in relation to its quality, it is considered to be using which type of strategy?

    1. Price dominant strategy
    2. Market Skimming strategy.
    3. Overcharging strategy.
    4. Snob strategy.

Chapter 3
MCQs of Marketing Mix

Answers Key

1. 4
2. 3
3. 3
4. 4
5. 1
6. 3
7. 3
8. 3
9. 1
10. 2
11. 2
12. 1
13. 3
14. 4
15. 4
16. 2
17. 2
18. 3
19. 1
20. 1
21. 2
22. 2
23. 4
24. 2

25. 2
26. 2
27. 1
28. 1
29. 3
30. 3
31. 1
32. 4
33. 2
34. 1
35. 3
36. 4
37. 3
38. 1
39. 1
40. 3

Chapter 4

MCQs Marketing Research

1. Marketing research can be described/defined as,

    1. Systematic gathering of data, recoding and analysis of data

    2. Providing information to take marketing decisions

    3. Both 1 and 2 are correct

    4. None of the above is correct

2. What are the types of data used in marketing research?

        1. Primary Data only

        2. Secondary date only

        3. Secondary and Primary data

        4. Secondary, Primary and Tertiary data

3. What is meant by primary data?

        1. Data that is freely available

        2. Data used by the company in the early stages of a research

        3. Fresh Data that is collected by the researcher specifically for this research

        4. Data that is reported in other research reports

4. What is meant by Secondary data?

        1. Data obtained in the latter part of the research

        2. Data gathered by company using its own research specifically for this research

        3. Data that is already available from other internal and external sources

        4. Data that is important to verify current findings

5. In the approach to research, the researcher should,

        1. First identify the data that is already available, study about it and complete the research

        2. Conduct a primary research to gather data for the

current research

3. Identify already available data and if that is not enough, then should proceed to collection of primary data

4. Conduct a pilot study to collect data before doing any of the above

6. Another name for Secondary Data is,

    1. Off the shelf data

    2. Old data

    3. Central Bank data

    4. Census and Statistics department data

7. The marketing manager instructs the researcher to refer to company sales records before embarking on research. What is he referring to?

    1. Primary Data

    2. Secondary Data

    3. Both Secondary and Primary Data

    4Data collected from a third party

8. Secondary data collection is,

    1. Is difficult to collect

    2. Is relatively expensive than the collection of Primary Data

3. Is relatively cheaper than the collection of Primary data

4. Requires specialized knowledge to analyze raw data

9. Which of the following statements is incorrect with regard to secondary data?

1. May not meet the specific needs of the current research

2. Accuracy of the data could be of concern

3. Date could be obsolete

4. Any data could be obtained through Secondary Data

10. If a researcher is conducting his data collection through observing the behavior of customers in a supermarket, what data is he collecting?

1. Secondary data

2. Primary data

3. Supermarket data

4. Fast Moving Consumer goods buying data

11. What is the most popular method of collecting primary data?

1. Observational method

2. Behavioral methods

3. Survey method

4. In depth Interview method

12. If a researcher is meeting people personally and asking questions about an issue, what kind of research is he doing?
    1. Survey
    2. In depth interview
    3. Observational
    4. Behavioral

13. If a researcher is conducting a research with small group of 12 people in an enclosed environment by asking questions, He is conducting,
    1. A survey
    2. A focus group study
    3. A Confidential research
    4. Research on personal preferences of a product

14. Which of the following statements is incorrect with regard primary data collection?
    1. It is cheaper to collect Primary data
    2. It is beneficial in collecting the most relevant data
    3. Accuracy can be relied upon
    4. Sufficient number of samples can be included.

15. First step in research process is to,
    1. Conduct a pilot study

2. Define the research problem

3. Collection of data

4. Develop a research plan

16. What is qualitative data?

1.. Data that can be easily counted

2. Data that describes about quality

3. Both above points 1 and 2

4. Data that cannot be counted in numbers

17. A researcher asks from a consumer; "how many time per month you visit this supermarket?". He is collecting,

1. Consumer Data

2. Quantitative Data

3. Qualitative Data

4. None of the above

18. There are two types of questions asked in a survey. These are,

1. Open ended and confidential

2. Close ended and difficult

3. Open ended and close ended

4. Easy questions and difficult questions

19. If a researcher asks, do you smoke or do not smoke, it is,

1. A Dichotomous question

2. A structured question

3. An unstructured question

4. A Likert scale question

20. Which one of the below are not considered as an internal company record?

1. Balance sheet

2. Annual report

3. Past research report by the company

4. Central Bank Report found in the company library

21. An option is given to answer a question as "Agree- Disagree- Neither". What type of a question is this?

1. It is Multiple Choice

2. It is a scale of importance

3. It is a Likert scale

4. It is a rating

22. An option is given to answer a question by selecting a scale a point on the scale as per opinion as "Tasty,…………………, Not tasty". What type of question is this?

1. It is a semantic differential

2. It is scale of importance

3. It is a rating

4. It is a Likert Scale

23. If a question is asked as "What do you think about the fast food served by us",

    1. It is an unstructured question

    2. It is a structured question

    3. It is a close end question

    4. It is a dichotomous question

24. When developing a questionnaire, one should not ask "catch all" questions. An example of a catch all question is,

    1. Were you able to catch all your customers by sending a flyer through an email?

    2. What is the best method you use to catch all your customers?

    3. Don't' you think that email marketing should be banned?

    4. Are you still smoking?

25. What is the logical procedure in selecting a sample?

    1. Identify the target population, decide on the number of people you need to study, select a sampling procedure

    2. Select a sampling procedure, select the target market and conduct a pilot study before commencing the major study

    3. Search how others have conducted research and

follow a method they have used to conduct a study similar to the issue you have

4. Find out how you your company has conducted research and follow that procedure

26. Probability sampling methods are,
   1. Quota sample, Convenient sample and simple random sample
   2. Judgement sample, Stratified random sample and cluster sample
   3. Simple random sample, Stratified random sample and quota sample
   4. Simple random sample, Stratified random sample and Cluster area sample

27. When every member of the population has an opportunity of being selected to the sample. It is called,
   1. Judgement sample
   2. Simple random sample
   3. Quota sample
   4. Cluster sample

28. If the population is divided into male and female groups and then samples are drawn from each group, it is called,

1. Quota sample
2. Stratified random sample
3. Cluster sample
4. Convenience sample

29. Data that is collected by an external firm or your firm for any other research other than the current research is called,

1. Primary data
2. Secondary date
3. Third party data
4. Exploratory

30. A company that is marketing sausages repeated a survey and found that the attitude towards consumption of sausages among the educated are negative. This suggests that the results are,

1. Predictable
2. Valid
3. Usable
4. Reliable

31. A new fruit juice is developed by company X, and they wish to undertake a survey. All the consumers in their target market would be the study's:

1. Population
2. Sample
3. Dependent Variable

4. Independent Variable

32. Company X needs to find out if their newly developed X mas card would be a hit in the market. They are at the end of November and do not have much time and resources to do the research. They will select ---------------- to conduct the research.
1. Post
2. Email
3. Personal interview
4. Telephone

33. Marketing research should provide information to,
1. Improve profits
2. Improve sales volume
3. Improve reduction in cost
4. Improve the ability of making correct decisions

34. Prior to embarking on a formal research to find the real cause of the drop in the sales of their soft drinks, the Marketing Manager of a company thinks that the drop was mainly due to the increased awareness among customers of problems associated with sugar in soft drinks. This is,
1. His opinion
2. His hypothesis

3. His idea

4. His interpretation

35. A Marketing manager observes that the sales of their Phone Model WWX has fallen by 20%. In what stage is he in the research process?

    1. Hypothesis development

    2. Problem identification

    3. Fact finding mission

    4. Sales data interpretation

36. If a soft drink company has collected data and is trying to assess and interpret what has happened to cause the drop in sales, it is called:

    1. Scanning of date

    2. tabulation of data

    3. Compiling data

    4. Analysis of data

37. So much of structured and unstructured data is collected by companies about various related and non-related personal and behavioral patterns of customers through different platforms.

    1. It is called inundation of data

    2. It is called a data mine

    3. It is called "big data"

    4. It is called "mega data"

38. Major criticism on "Big Data" is that it,
    1. Is Extremely difficult to analyze
    2. Is a Security and privacy issue
    3. Is Not suitable to understand complex customer behavior
    4. Is takes up too much storage

39. Loyalty cards issued by companies not only ensure repeat customers but establish an easy mode of,
    1. Trapping the customers
    2. Conducting research on the buyer behavior through the study of their purchase records
    3. Developing a competitive advantage
    4. Making customers buy unnecessary products

40. If a marketing company decides to outsource its research task, which of the following is not a major criterion:
    1. The agency's past record
    2. The size of the agency
    3. The urgency of the research
    4. Expertise required to conduct the research

41. Exploratory research means,
    1. Seeking to discover the cause of a specific problem

by discussing the issue with informed sources both internal and external parties

2. Examining data from other information sources

3. Both above 1 and 2 are correct

4. Only 1 above is correct

42. What is a hypothesis in marketing research?

1. Tentative explanation for some specific issue

2. Mathematical model that could be tested through a statistical package

3. Marketers imagination for some specific issue

4. A theory to be tested in a marketing research

43. What is data mining?

1. It is a method of searching through computerized data files to detect patterns

2. It is an attempt to fish out the relevant data from huge pile of data

3. Sifting both secondary and primary data collected for the research

4. Obtaining data through decades of past internal company data.

44. Business intelligence is the process of ………………………….. it to improve business strategy, tactics and regular operations.

1. Gathering information and recording
2. Gathering information and analyzing
3. Using agents to gather competitor's information and reporting
4. Using Intelligent Business Analysts to gather different sources of information

45. A marketer in the modern day should have a ………………………………… that consists of software that helps users in the decision making process to obtain and apply information for effective decision making.

    1. Business Intelligence System (BIS)
    2. Marketing Information System (MIS)
    3. Marketing Decision Support System (MDSS)
    4. Data Reporting System (DRS)

46. In sales forecasting, a system called ……………………………… that combines and averages the outlook of top executives from areas such as marketing, production, finance etc. is used. It is called,

    1. Delphi Technique
    2. Expert Opinion
    3. Executives view
    4. Jury of Executive Opinion (Jury Method)

47. In sales forecasting, a system that gathers and redistributes

several rounds of anonymous forecasting until the participants come to a consensus is called,

    1. Delphi Technique

    2. Circulation Method

    3. Sales Force Composite

    4. Jury of Executive Opinion (Jury Method)

48. ………………………… is a sales forecasting method used to forecast the sales by adding up
individual sales agent's/representatives forecasts for sales in their assigned sales territories? It is called the "bottom up approach" in sales forecasting.

    1. Simple Technique

    2. Cumulative Method

    3. Sales Force Composite

    4. Overall approach

49. A quantitative Technique in sales forecasting is called ……………………………. This gives a weightage to each year of sales, giving a greater weight to sales from the most recent years in analyzing the trend in sales.

    1. Trend Analysis

    2. Exponential Smoothing

    3. Demand Measurement

    4. Market Analytics

50. A market research that observes a customer or group of customers in their natural setting and interprets their behavior on their social and cultural attributes is called,

1. Interpretative or ethnographic research
2. Social research
3. Cultural research
4. In depth research

Chapter 4
MCQs Marketing Research

Answers Key
1. 4
2. 3
3. 3
4. 3
5. 3
6. 1
7. 2
8. 3
9. 4
10. 2
11. 3
12. 1
13. 2
14. 1
15. 2

16. 4
17. 2
18. 3
19. 1
20. 4
21. 3
22. 1
23. 1
24. 4
25. 1
26. 4
27. 3
28. 2
29. 2
30. 4
31. 1
32. 2
33. 4
34. 2
35. 2
36. 4
37. 3
38. 2
39. 2
40. 2
41. 4
42. 1
43. 1
44. 2
45. 3
46. 4
47. 1
48. 3

49. 2
50. 1

Chapter 5
MCQs on Consumer Behavior

1. Consumer behavior is,

    1. How a consumer buys goods and services

    2. Study of activities of consumer in decision making in buying, consuming and disposing

    3. How a consumer reacts to promotion and publicity

    4. Study of attitude towards buying goods and services

2. A ………… between the current status and the desired status needs to be studied when offering goods to consumers.

        1. Need

        2. Want

        3. Discrepancy

        4. Gap

3. When there is a need the consumer can,

        1. Look for means of satisfying need

        2. Suppress the need

        3. Do either of 1 or 2 above

        4. Can postpone the need

4. Maslow did research on how humans,

        1. Behave in the market place

        2. Satisfy their needs

        3. Compete with each other in obtaining their needs

        4. Desires are different from each other

5. Maslow found that humans have,

        1. Simple to complex needs

        2. Different needs at any given time

        3. Natural instinct to buy goods and service of high quality

        4. A trend in fulfilling different needs at the same

time

6. Maslow's needs hierarchy in logical order is as follows,
    1. Social needs, physiological needs, esteem needs, self-actualization needs and safety needs
    2. Safety needs, physiological needs, esteem needs, social needs and self-actualization needs
    3. Physiological needs, esteem needs, safety needs, social needs and self-actualization needs
    4. Physiological needs, safety needs, social needs, esteem needs and self-actualization needs

7. As per Maslow, the physiological needs are;
    1. Food and shelter
    2. Secured means of living and employment
    3. Love and affection
    4. Social recognition

8. Maslow says that at self-actualization level of needs,
    1. Humans are more concerned about needs of others
    2. Humans are more concerned about fulfilling their potential
    3. Humans are more considered about social recognition
    4. Humans are more concerned about developing relationships

9. The main difference between needs and wants is that,

    1. Needs are unlimited and wants are limited

    2. Wants are unlimited and needs are limited

    3. Wants are the means of expressing a need

    4. Both above 2 and 3 are correct

10 Demand for marketers' products are created by,

    1. Customers who have needs

    2. Customers whose need is backed by purchasing power

    3. Customers whose need is backed by purchasing power plus authority to buy

    4. Customers who have disposable income

11. Marketers have to address needs of both customer and consumer,

    1. When the product is a luxury item

    2. When the product is wanted by one person but purchased by another person

    3. When a product is a fast moving consumer product

    4. When the product is an innovative product

12. A newly established plastic bottle manufacturing factory seeks to buy raw materials. It is a,

1. Straight rebuy purchase
2. Delayed purchase
3. New-task purchase
4. Modified rebuy purchase

13. While buying bread and sugar which kind of behavior is displayed by a person?

1. Extensive problem-solving behavior
2. Routinized buying behavior
3. Variety seeking behavior
4. Outward information-seeking behavior

14. Buying goods for further processing or for use in the production process refers to which of the following markets?

1. Consumer markets
2. Processing markets
3. Resales markets
4. Business markets

15. Main focus of Consumer behavior is the study of how any type of consumer,

1. Buys goods in a supermarket
2. Buys any type of goods and services in any type of market
3. Buys or sells goods and services in any type of market

4. Buys consumer goods in any market.

16. The basic five-stage model of the consumer buying behavior includes all of the following stages other than ....

1. Observation of how others buy
2. Problem recognition
3. Information search
4. Purchase decision

17. Elements that would decide the consumer value are,

1. Comparison of benefits of other products in the market with the product purchased
2. Benefits and cost of the product
3. Expectation of the customer and the satisfaction received
4. Money saved by non-purchase of the price of competitive products

18. While buying bread and sugar which type of information is searched by the buyer?

1. Internal search
2. External search
3. Both above 1 and 2
4. Mainly above 1

19. A need of a customer may arise as an internal stimulus or and of an external stimulus. In marketing, this is called,

    1. Buying signal

    2. Problem recognition

    3. Cognitive dissonance

    4. Purchase decision

20. Although you bought a phone by paying a higher price, the rejected lower priced one has better picture quality in the camera. You are asking a question from yourself, "Have I taken the correct decision?". In marketing this is called,

    1. Consumer confusion

    2. Consumer dilemma

    3. Cognitive dissonance

    4. Marketing myopia

21. Business to business market is called B 2 B market. It buys products mainly to,

    1. Use for their day to day consumption

    2. Use to produce goods and service and resell

    3. Produce goods and services to end users such as householders

    4. Produce goods and service to sell it to other businesses

22. In a business, usually one individual does not take buying decisions. They have few more persons in the decision-making process. In marketing jargon, it is called,

    1. Purchasing Board
    2. Decision Making Unit (DMU)
    3. Buying Committee
    4. Tender Board

23. In a typical Decision Making Unit, following members are found:

    1. Manager, Buyer, Gatekeepers and Technical Expert
    2. Users, Influencers, Buyers, Deciders and Gatekeepers
    3. Directors, Managers, Accountant and Engineers
    4. Managers, Auditors, Technical Experts and Users

24. If a person in the Decision Making Unit can regulate the flow of information from suppliers that comes to the DMU, he or she is called,

    1. Regulator
    2. Auditor
    3. Gatekeeper
    4. Purchasing Officer

25. The logical order of a typical organizational buying process would be,

1. Need description- Supplier search- Proposal solicitation- supplier selection- purchase and performance review
2. Problem recognition- Need Description-Product specification- supplier selection- supplier selection- purchase and performance review
3. Product specification- Need recognition- Problem recognition- supplier search – Order and performance review
4. Product specification- supplier search- evaluation – purchase and performance review

26. Consumers think and learn about products and services in the marketplace by,

1. Cognition, Perceptions and Learning
2. Cognition, Attitudes, and World View
3. Perceptions, Attitudes and Opinions
4. Communication, Observation and Learning

27. When consumers buy products that are in the higher-end and that they regularly do not buy, they consult their friends

and relatives. This behavior is called,
1. Seeking Outsider views
2. Seeking Reference group opinion
3. Consultative buying
4. Extended learning

28. In the modern day, buyer's decision making process is also called as "proposition acquisition process" and it has the following distinct steps:
1. Motive development or need recognition, Information search, information evaluation, selection, purchase and post purchase evaluation
2. Motive development or need recognition, Information search, information evaluation, perception, selection, purchase and post purchase evaluation
3. Motive development or need recognition, Information search, information evaluation, attitude formation, purchase and post purchase evaluation
4. Motive development or need recognition, environment scanning, Information search, information evaluation, selection, purchase and post purchase evaluation

29. Personality determines how we respond to our environment in a relatively stable way over a time. There are various theories

of personality. A theory which is concerned with how we perceive ourselves as consumers is described in,

    1. The psychoanalytic approach
    2. Trait Theory
    3. Behavioral Theory
    4. Self-concept Theory

30. Which of the following would correctly be named as a cultural factor that would influence consumer buyer behavior?

    1. Family
    2. Social class
    3. Lifestyle
    4. Reference group

31. Cognitive dissonance occurs in which stage of the buyer decision making process model?

    1. Need recognition
    2. Information search
    3. Evaluation of alternatives
    4. Post purchase behavior

32. The -----------------is a person within a reference group who, because of special skills, knowledge, personality, or other characteristics, exerts influence on others.

1. Facilitator
2. Referent actor
3. Opinion leader
4. Social role player

33. ------------describes changes in an individual's behavior arising from experience.
1. Maslow
2. Motivation
3. Perception
4. Learning

34. Technological advances, shifts in consumer preferences, and increased competition, all of which reduce demand for a product are typical of which stage in the PLC?
1. Decline stage
2. Introduction stage
3. Growth stage
4. Maturity stage

35. In a consumer survey, the-------------method asks the consumer to rank three items in order of preference. These are:
1. Rank-order
2. Focus group
3. Monadic-rating
4. Likert scale

36. Customers buy from stores and firms that offer the highest---------.

    1. Customer perceived value

    2. Care for environment

    3. Product image

    4. Number of features and benefits

37. ----------------is the effect one person has on another's attitude or purchase
probability.

    1. Personal influence

    2. Effective influence

    3. Direct influence

    4. Market influence

38. In response to mega supermarkets, entrepreneurial retailers are
building entertainment into stores with coffee bars, lectures, demonstrations, and
performances. They are marketing a/an----------------rather than a product assortment.

    1. Experience

    2. Customer value

3. Customer delight

4. Total service solution

39. What do you mean by evoked set?

1. All the alternative products that a buyer considers in a purchasing decision

2. Number of selected alternatives that a consumer considers in making a purchasing decision

3. The items that consumer has a personal interest

4. The items that consumer has set aside as non-interest products

40. Goods like chocolates are kept by the side of the teller's counter in most of the supermarkets. Why?

1. They are impulsive goods

2. They are goods for kids

3. They are goods that are low in price

4. They are kept to give it away as cash when coins are in short supply to give the balance money to the consumers.

41. A model used in studying of the buying behaviour of consumers; assumes that what takes place in the ……………………….of the consumer's mind can be inferred from the study of observed stimuli and responses.

1. Perception

2. Status
3. Cognition
4. Black Box

42. **A culture of consumers has a major influence on their buying behavior. A culture can be described as,**
    1. Traditional customs, songs, dances and languages
    2. Values, beliefs. preferences handed down from generations and taste and experiences
    3. The perception of different ethnic communities about the world and its surroundings
    4. Distinct modes of behavior of different ethnic and religious groups within a society

43. **Each culture has number of micro cultures: groups with their unique behaviors. Understanding such cultures,**
    1. Is not an easy task and it is a futile effort to do so
    2. It is a very sensitive issue and marketers may not attempt to use such behavior for their advantage
    3. Understanding such cultures can help marketers develop more effective marketing strategies
    4. Since it is difficult to predict behavior of such micro cultures marketers should not study them in detail

44. ………………………… means what a person attributes to incoming stimuli gathered through the five senses.

        1. Attitude
        2. Perception
        3. Cognition
        4. Self-concept

45. ………………………………….. of an object or event results from the interaction of two types of factors: Stimulus factors and Individual factors.

        1. Understanding
        2. Cognition
        3. Perception
        4. Learning

46. A person's reactions when enduring favourable or unfavourable evaluations, emotions, or action tendencies toward some object or idea is called,

        1. Perception
        2. Learning
        3. Attitude
        4. Behavior

47. Cognition, affective and behavioral are components of ………………………………..

1. Attitude
2. Learning
3. Perception
4. Response

48. Learning in marketing context refers to immediate or expected changes in consumer behavior as a result of experience. Fear, greed, pride, thirst, pain avoidance and rivalry are components of the learning process. It is called,

1. Drives
2. Response
3. Motivators
4. Influencers

49. What are the components of person's self –concept theory?

1. Self –image, real-self, ideal self, looking glass-self
2. Active –self, inactive-self, emotional self, social-self
3. Negative-self, Positive- self, Narrow- self, broader-self
4. Aggressive-self, Non aggressive-self, Open- self, closed- self

50. The way that an individual thinks others see him or her is called,

1. Real Self

2. Looking glass- self

3. Ideal-self

4. Self-image

51. Business to Business (B 2 B) markets are segmented on following criteria;

1. Demographic, Geographic, Customer type and Psychographic

2. Demographic, Purchase categories, Customer type, end user application

3. Geographic, Personality, Customer type, end user application

4. Centralized, De centralized, Services, manufacturing

52. In Business to Business (B 2 B) markets one of the segmentation criteria is demographic characteristics. In this criteria, firms can be grouped,

1. By size, sales revenue and number of employees etc.

2. By manufacturer, service provider, not for profit organization, wholesaler or retailer

3. By the location of the businesses such as North, South, East and West regions

4. By the buyer categories such as centralized and localized purchases

53. Basis for segmentation by ……………………………………. in Business to Business (B 2 B) markets, focuses on the precise way in which a business purchaser will ……………….. a product

        1. Demographic - manufacture

        2. Purchase categories - buy

        3. End user application - use

        4. How purchases are made - pay price for

54. In comparison to consumer markets, Business to Business markets are

        1. More geographically concentrated

        2. Demand is relatively inelastic

        3. None of the above is correct

        4. Both 1 and 2 are correct

55. Business to Business markets has a derived demand. Derived demand,

        1. Has a link on the demand for marketers output (manufactured services or products)

        2. Affects the capital items and expense items

        3. Both above 1 and 2 are correct

        4. Both above 1 and 2 are wrong

56. Both cement and sand are required to build most homes and

business premises. If the cement supply falls it is very likely that demand for sand also will be negatively affected. This is called,

    1. Volatile demand
    2. Derived demand
    3. Inelastic demand
    4. Joint demand

57. In recent years, there has been a growing trend in obtaining certain services and products from outside of national boundaries of companies to improve efficiency and cut costs. As a result, some new terms added to the business lexicon were:

    1. Outsourcing, multiple sourcing, offshoring
    2. Outsourcing, nearshoring, offshoring
    3. Contact supplying, component manufacturing, remanufacturing
    4. Just in time, Soul sourcing, Asian sourcing

58. Buying from suppliers who are also customers, is called,

    1. Straight rebuy
    2. Collaborative buying
    3. Reciprocity buying
    4. Relationship buying

59. ……………………….. contributes to the buying decision process in a Business to Business environment, by supplying

information on how to evaluate alternative products and setting buying specifications.

1. Deciders
2. Managers
3. influencers
4. Buyers

60. Although .... are one of the largest single buyers of products and services in any country, generally not much attention is given in marketing literature for their buyer behavior.

1. Multinationals
2. Governments
3. NGOs
4. Military

Chapter 5
MCQs on Consumer Behavior

Answers Key
1. 2
2. 4
3. 3
4. 2
5. 1
6. 4
7. 1

8. 2
9. 4
10. 3
11. 2
12. 3
13. 2
14. 4
15. 2
16. 1
17. 2
18. 4
19. 2
20. 3
21. 2
22. 1
23. 2
24. 3
25. 2
26. 1
27. 2
28. 1
29. 4
30. 2
31. 4
32. 3
33. 4
34. 1
35. 1
36. 1
37. 1
38. 1
39. 2
40. 1
41. 4
42. 2
43. 3
44. 3
45. 3
46. 1

47. 1
48. 1
49. 3
50. 2
51. 2
52. 1
53. 3
54. 4
55. 3
56. 4
57. 2
58. 3
59. 3
60. 2

Chapter 6

MCQs on Segmenting, Targeting and

Positioning

1. What are markets?
    1. A geographical place where buyers and sellers gather
    2. Open places where anybody can buy and sell
    3. People with needs and wants, willing to buy them and have the ability buy and connect with sellers
    4. Competitive place where sellers try to persuade buyers buy their products

2. Which one of the following is untrue?
    1. Markets could be present market or future markets
    2. Markets may have customers and consumers
    3. Markets could be past market or present market
    4. Markets could comprise of individuals or organizations

3. If a company designs a product to appeal to larger number of buyers and uses channels of advertising that covers a larger audience,
    1. It is offering a product to the Mass Market
    2. It is offering a product to a segment of the market
    3. It is offering a product to a niche market
    4. It is offering a product to General Market

4. One of the issues with offering a product in general for a mass

market is,

    1. A company cannot have a higher profit margin

    2. A company will have to mark very competitive price

    3. A company will have issues with distribution

    4. A company may not be able to compete with more focused competitors who supply different types of products

5. Segmentation is,

    1. Identifying customer groups

    2. Categorizing customers as per their ability to purchase

    3. Classifying customers into prospects and non-prospects

    4. Classifying customers with similar needs and wants

6. Mass customization is,

    1. Identifying each and everyone's need separately and serve different products to them

    2. Understanding the customers in a larger market

    3. Offering a common product to all the customers

    4. Distributing products in mass scale

7. Segmentation comes in between,

    1. Mass market and Niche market

2. Mass market and Competitive market

3. Mass market and Mass customization

4. Competitive market and non- competitive market

8. Which one of the following statements is untrue with regard to Niche market?

1. A niche market more narrowly defines group, seeking distinctive mix of benefits

2. Niche market mainly exists for luxury goods

3. It is typically a small market whose needs are served in a segmented market

4. Niche market could be identified within a segment by sub dividing the segment again

9. Ultimate level of segmentation is to,

1. Have one customer per segment

2. Have only the high buying potential customers

3. Have customers always loyal to the company products

4. Have customers who buy their products frequently

10. Benefits of segmentation allows to,

1. Understand the customer better

2. Understand the competitor better

3. Both 1 and 2 are incorrect

4. Both 1 and 2 above are true

11. If a market is segmented well it should be,

    1. Measurable, substantial, accessible and differentiable

    2. Measurable, accessible and profitable

    3. Meaningful, manageable, and accessible

    4. Measurable, understandable and controllable

12. Geographic segmentation is dividing the market into categories such as,

    1. Nationality, Countries, Regions and Density

    2. Countries, Regions, Religion and Family Size

    3. Countries, Regions, Density and Climate

    4. North- South, Cold- Topical and Generation

13. Family size and occupation fall under,

    1. Demographic segmentation

    2. Demographic and geographic segmentation

    3. Psychological segmentation

    4. Behavioral segmentation

14. A company wants to carry out segmentation on the criteria of benefit and occasion. This is,

    1. Psychological segmentation

    2. Behavioral segmentation

   3. Demographic segmentation

   4. Demographic and psychological segmentation

15. Psychographic segmentation takes the following into consideration:

   1. Life Style, Attitudes, Values and Personality

   2. Generation and Religion

   3. Benefit and Occasion

   4. Social Class and Level of Education

16. Criteria for behavioral (product related) segmentation includes,

   1. Quality, Service, Durability and Convenience Seekers

   2. Usage Status, Usage Rate, State of Readiness to Buy

   3. Attitude towards a product such as Positive, Negative, Indifferent or Hostile

   4. All of the above

17. Logical sequence target market selection is,

   1. Segmenting, targeting and understanding the whole market

   2. Understanding market, segmentation and targeting

   3. Targeting, segmentation and understanding the market

4. Positioning, Targeting and Segmentation

18. Once the segmentation is done, a marketer can offer products to,
        1. Single segment
        2. Selective segments
        3. Full market
        4. All of the above

19. If a marketer is offering different products to different segments, the marketer is concentrating on,
        1. Single segment
        2. Selective specialization
        3. Product specialization
        4. Market specialization

20. Benz is offering luxury cars to the markets all over the world. It is,
        1. Market specialization
        2. Product specialization
        3. Single segmentation
        4. Full market coverage

21. Positioning is,
        1. Act of creating a perception or image or status in the buyer's mind

2. Placing products in a place where customers can see it very well

3. Promoting the product where more customers get exposed

4. Both above 2 and 3

22. Which of the following will Perceptual map provide?

1. Perception of the customers only to your product

2. Perception of customers in the market for competitive products only

3. Perception of customers in the market for all the products

2. Competitive advantage your product is having over the others

23. Positioning is,

1. A Strategic activity

2. Aimed at developing a sustainable competitive advantage

3. Both 1 and 2 are correct

2. None of the above is correct

24. During the period 1946 to 1964, almost 77 million babies were born in the United States alone, comprising nearly 40% of the American population. This demographic group is popularly known as,

1. Generation X
2. Generation Y
3. Baby Boomers
4. None of the above

25. If customers are targeted at very narrow basic levels, such as by the postal code, specific occupation, or lifestyles, it is called,

1. Mass customization
2. Micro marketing
3. Niche marketing
4. None of the above

26. BMW uses a tag line the "Ultimate driving machine". This is part of its,

1. Advertising strategy
2. Positioning strategy
3. Product strategy
4. Competitive strategy

27. Group born between 1966 and 1981 are called,

1. Generation Y
2. Generation X
3. Generation M
4. Baby boomers

28. The tendency of a members of a group to be influenced and

bound together by events occurring during their key formative years- roughly 17 to 22 years of age, is called,

    1. Cohort effect
    2. Social effect
    3. Generation effect
    4. Youth effect

29. The above age group (roughly 17-22 years of age) is categorized differently than Generation Y, Millennials, Generation Next and Echo boomers. They are commonly identified as,

    1. Video game generation
    2. High Tech generation
    3. Social media generation
    4. Instant message loving generation

30. According to ………………….. , when the household income increases, a smaller percentage of expenditure goes for food, the percentage spent on housing and clothing remains constant but percentage spent on other items such as recreation increases.

    1. Maslow's needs hierarchy
    2. Ansof's matrix
    3. Engel's law
    4. Seth Godin

31. In developing psychographic profiles, large scale surveys are conducted. Mostly they ask consumers about,

       1. Activities, interest and opinions

       2. Family, education and occupation

       3. Income, savings and spending patterns

       4. Ethnicity, religion and beliefs

32. This psychographic segmentation system divides consumers into eight psychographic categories: innovators, thinkers, achievers, experiencers, believers, strivers, makers and survivors. This segmentation system is called,

       1. Attitudes and Values (AALS)

       2. Values and Lifestyle (VALS)

       3. Status and Expectations (SES)

       4. Issues and Challenges (ICS)

33. Although no one can suggest that psychographic segmentation is an exact science, it does help marketers to,

       1. Predict consumers spending behavior in a target market

       2. Quantify aspects of consumer's personalities and lifestyle to create good and services for a target market

       3. Understand the buyer behavior of consumers in a target market

       4. Influence the perception of consumers to buy its

products and services in a given market

34. One of the criteria used in behavioral or product related segmentation is usage rate. In general, relatively few heavy uses of a product can count for much of its revenue. This phenomenon is in line with,

1. Pareto's 80/ 20 rule
2. Maslow hierarchy
3. Porters Five forces
4. Pareto's 70/30 rule

35. A combination of demographic and psychographic segmentation will,

1. Confuse the marketer
2. Make the marketer understand the market better
3. Confuse the consumer
4. Make the consumer understand the marketer's tactics

36. Socio- Economic classification (segmentation) is based on two parameters:

1. Education and Occupation
2. Wealth and Income
3. Social status and Age
4. Education and Expenditure

37. What is the most common basis used to segment consumer markets?

   1. Psychographic
   2. Behavioral
   3. Demographic
   4. Geographic

38 Hedonic consumption is defined as the multisensory, fantasy, and emotional aspects of consumers' interactions with products. It involves use of a product to fulfill fantasies and satisfy emotions. Which of the following is the investigation of the hedonic consumption of products?

   1. Experiential consumption
   2. Expectation dimension
   3. Experimental perspective
   4. Social perspective

39. At the outsell of market segmentation process, a marketer should,

   1. Consult a segmentation expert to get advice
   2. Allocate a budget for segmentation
   3. Understand the criteria used for segmentation
   4. Understand how competitors have made their segmentation

40. In demographic segmentation, what can be understood through the study of the family life cycle?

    1. Process of family formation, its composition and dissolution

    2. The development of income within the family

    3. The members who would take buying decisions in a family

    4. The relationships among different members of the family and how they will buy products

Chapter 6

MCQs on Segmenting, Targeting and Positioning

Answer
1. 3
2. 3
3. 1
4. 4
5. 4
6. 1
7. 2
8. 2
9. 1
10. 4
11. 1
12. 3.
13. 1

14. 2
15. 1
16. 4
17. 2
18. 4
19. 2
20. 2
21. 1
22. 3
23. 3
24. 3
25. 2
26. 2
27. 2
28. 1
29. 1
30. 3
31. 1
32. 2
33. 2
34. 1
35. 2
36. 1
37. 3
38. 1
39. 3
40. 1

Chapter 7
MCQs on Product Decisions

1. A "product" could be defined as,

1. Anything that can be offered to a market to satisfy a want or a need
2. Products and services that are offered to consumers
3. Various types of goods and service available in the market
4. Items that can be seen and touched

2. A product could be a physical product, place, organization, idea, person or a service. When a famous football player is marketed by his manager to the commercial world to appear in advertisements, it is called,

1. Service
2. Physical product
3. Idea
4. Person

3. A product has three major aspects:

1. Size, Shape and Color
2. Package, Content and Flavor
3. Physical, Functional and Symbolic Aspects
4. Advertised, Presented and Delivered

4. In a tooth paste what is the symbolic aspect of the product?

1. It is a tooth paste
2. It cleans teeth
3. It whitens e teeth

        4. It helps reduce tooth decay

5. According to Phillip Kotler, product has five levels:
        1. Outer Package, Inner Package, Contents, Taste and Nutrition
        2. Core, Generic, Expected, Augmented and Potential
        3. Development, Introductory, Growth, Maturity and Decline
        4. Durability, Perishability, Inseparability, Intangibility and Variability

6. In the tangibility continuum, what could be identified as a pure tangible product?
        1. Sermon in a church/ temple/ Kovil
        2. Service in a salon
        3. Service in a hospital
        4. Service in a restaurant

7. What could be identified as hybrid (50% to 50%) tangible and intangible goods?
        1. Airline ticket
        2. Ticket to a musical show
        3. Service in a restaurant
        4. Service in a salon

8. What product could be identified as a major intangible

product with minor tangible product?

    1. Airline service

    2. Restaurant service

    3. A car

    4. Pencil

9. One of the famous definition of brandings is: Name, term, sign, symbol or design or a combination of them to identify the goods and services of one seller or group of sellers and ………………………………… from those of competitors.

    1. Highlight

    2. Differentiate

    3. Juxtapose

    4. Attracted

10. Which one of the following statements is wrong as to the importance of branding to consumers?

    1. Makes easy to identify

    2. Reduces risk in purchasing

    3. Helps buying nutritious products

    4. Helps product evaluation

11. If branding allows differentiation, targeting and positioning and defend against competition, who will benefit?

    1. Retailer

    2. Wholesaler

3. Manufacture

4. Retailer and wholesaler

12. Brand equity is,

1. Brand value indicated in the balance sheet of the manufacture
2. Brand value given by branding valuing organizations
3. Value given to a brand by the customers on their perspective
3. Price of the product divided by the value of benefits

13. Logical sequence of brand development process is:

1. Brand recognition, brand acceptance, brand preference and brand loyalty
2. Brand acceptance, brand recognition, brand preference and brand loyalty
3. Brand preference, brand recognition, brand preference and brand loyalty
3. Brand exposure, brand acceptance, brand preference and brand loyalty

14. Companies like Unilever, Proctor and Gamble and HP use…………………….. for their products.

1. Individual brand names

2. Family brand names

3. Multi-level brand names

4. Corporate name

15. Companies like Toyota Motor Corporation use branding strategies like Toyota- Corolla, Toyota –Corona, Toyota – Prius, Toyota –Hilux: they are using.

1. Individual brand names

2. Family brand names

3. Multi-level brand names

4. Corporate name and individual brand names

16. What is common in brand names like Altus, Sprite, Nike, Apollo?

1. They are Greek Heroes

2. They are Greek Gods

3. They are names of fables

4. They are names of epic stories

17. There is a tendency in naming the brand with an inherent quality, utility value of technology of the product such as Mobitel, Celltel, Tropicana, Suntec, Air Canada: the advantage of doing so is,

1. It makes it easy for the customer to remember

2. It makes it easy for the marketer to advertise and describe the product

3. It makes it easy for the marketer to distinguish the product form competitors' products

4. It makes it easy to register as a trade mark

18. Most important elements in naming a brand are,

1. It should be easy to pronounce and remember
2. It should be protectable, adaptable and distinguishable
3. None of the above is correct
4. Above 1 and 2 both together are correct

19. Although packaging is fundamentally used for protecting the product from elements form the environment, now it is mainly seen as a,

1. Fashion
2. Silent salesman
3. Environment friendly element
4. Innovation to make user friendly products

20. Product life cycle theory generally assumes that a product,

1. Has three stages of life
2. Has a very short life in the market
3. Has life cycle from conception to decline
4. Has a life cycle that cannot be predicted

21. If sales and profits are low, distribution is with few, the cost

of promotion is relatively high and the risk of failure is also high: What is the stage of the product as per the product life cycle theory?

1. Development stage
2. Introductory stage
3. Growth stage
4. Maturity Stage

22. If competitors are watching whether to enter the market or not: what is the stage of the product as per the product life cycle theory?

1. Development stage
2. Growth stage
3. Introductory stage
4. Maturity Stage

23. If many changes are required to be made into the marketing mix to be afloat on the market, what is the stage of the product as per the product life cycle theory?

1. Development stage
2. Growth stage
3. Introductory stage
4. Maturity Stage

24. If competitors do not enter the market and distributors are giving up distribution, what is the stage of the product as per the

product life cycle theory?

    1. Development stage

    2. Growth stage

    3. Decline stage

    4. Maturity Stage

25. If there are many competitors in the market and profit margins are low but the sales volume is high, what is the stage of the product as per the product life cycle theory?

    1. Development stage

    2. Growth stage

    3. Decline stage

    4. Maturity Stage

26. If a product shoots up in the market within a very short period of introduction and subsequently drops to a very low level of sales or even goes out of demand, what do you call such products?

    1. Fashion Items

    2. Fad items

    3. Come and go items

    4. Cheap quality items

27. One of the major drawbacks of the Product Life Cycle (PLC) theory is,

    1. Stages of PLC are difficult to distinguish,

identifying where one stage ends and the other begins is very difficult

2. PLC is not very useful

3. PLC does not show the path of a product

4. PLC is not a tool for forecasting and strategic planning

28. "Introducing new products is an essential tactical activity",

    1. True

    2. False

29. Types of new products could be categorized into:

    1. High- tech and conventional products

    2. Innovative, replacement and imitative products

    3. Durable and non- durable products

    4. Consumer and industrial products

30. If a product is truly new to the customers and it provides a completely different alternative to existing products. It is called,

    1. High-tech product

    2. Consumer friendly product

    3. Innovative product

    4. Replacement product

31. Digital phones made analogue phones obsolete as disposable

racers did for conventional blade base racers. They are,

    1. Innovative products

    2. High tech products

    3. Imitative products

    4. Replacement products

32. Big majority of the new products introduced to the market are,

    1. Innovative products

    2. High tech products

    3. Imitative products

    4. Replacement products

33. In new product development process, the customer need will be identified through ……………… analysis.

    1. Gap

    2. Michael Porter

    3. Market

    4. Customer

34. If there is a need of the customer not served by the marketer, marketer can,

    1. Introduce new products

    2. Make improvements in existing products

    3. Make improvement in supporting services

    4. All of the above

35. Logical order of proper new product development would be:

1. Idea generation, Idea screening, Business analysis, Concept development, Test Marketing, Product development, Marketing Strategy and Commercialization
2. Idea generation, Idea screening, Business analysis, Product development, Concept development, Test Marketing, Marketing Strategy and Commercialization
3. Idea generation, Idea screening, Concept development, Business analysis, Test Marketing, Product development, Marketing Strategy and Commercialization
4. Idea generation, Idea screening, Concept development, Marketing Strategy, Business analysis, Product development, Test Marketing and Commercialization

36. Most of the new ideas are generated by,

1. Customers
2. Outside inventors
3. Internal staff
4. Consultants

37. A new idea has to be developed into a concept. It must be tested within a sample of customers before taking any other step. Therefore, product concept should,

    1. Provide a detailed version of the idea stated in meaningful consumer terms

    2. Provide features and benefits with technical specs

    3. Provide an actual sample of the product should be shown

    4. Provide the new technology used

38. In developing marketing strategies for a new product, a marketer should concentrate mainly on,

    1. Commercial performance and profit estimates

    2. Product, Price, Promotion and Place Strategies

    3. Direct and indirect competitors

    4. Resources required and risk involved

39. In the business analysis for a new product, the marketer's primary concern would be to find out,

    1. Cost estimation

    2. Asses the risk involved

    3. Estimate the overall commercial performance of the proposed product

4. Product, Price, Place and Promotion strategies

40. A "prototype" of a product is,
1. Developing an actual sample of the product that would be marketed
2. Generally developed by the research and development section
3. Both above 1 and 2 are correct
4. None of the above is correct

41. In test marketing a product, the product will be,
1. Sold at a discounted price
2. Sold at the expected price, in a limited area where the marketer can measure the response
3. Sold only to its members of the staff
4. Given to consumer authorities to check the suitability of the product to be sold to consumers

42. Ideally the test marketing should be done in a market where it reflects……………………………….
1. The features and benefits well.
2. The unique technology that the competitors would not be able to copy within a short period of time.
3. The target market that the product to be launched.
4. The nature of the products that are introduced by the marketer for the competition.

43. A major concern about conducting a test market of a product is to,

    1. Find out the acceptance of features and benefits of the product by the consumers

    2. Find out the demand for the product

    3. Evaluate the reaction of the competitors

    4. Evaluate all the elements of the marketing mix

44. Purpose of conducting a test market is to,

    1. Show the competitors about the strength of the marketer in developing new products and impending challenge they will face

    2. Show customers that the marketer is always leading the race in developing products

    3. Determine how the marketing mix should be adjusted before a full scale launch of the new product

    4. Showcase the new technologies that marketer incorporates in future products

45. In what circumstances should conducting a test market for a product be avoided or only restricted to staff members only?

    1. When the cost of the product is high

    2. When the cost of test marketing is high

    3. When the product could easily be copied by the competitors

4. Cannot find a suitable sample of customers to test market the product

46. What should a marketer do first before launching (commercializing) a product to the market?

    1. Determine the method of launch

    2. Let the companywide employees know about the product and it features

    3. Have a press conference

    4. Distribute promotional material among the distributors

47. The assortment of product lines and individual product offerings are called:

    1. Product mix

    2. Product mix depth

    3. Product mix width

    4. Product mix variety

48. The number of different products a firm sell is called:

    1. Product mix length

    2. Product mix depth

    3. Product mix width

    4. Product mix variety

49. The variation in each product that the firm markets in a product is called:

1. Product mix length
2. Product mix depth
3. Product mix width
4. Product mix variety

50. Development of individual offerings that appeal to different market segments while remaining closely related to the existing product line is called:

1. Product mix extension
2. Product depth diversification
3. Product line extension
4. Product differentiation

Chapter 7
MCQs on Product Decisions

Answer Key
1. 1
2. 4
3. 3
4. 4
5. 2
6. 1
7. 3
8. 1

9. 2
10. 3
11. 3
12. 3
13. 1
14. 1
15. 4
16. 2
17. 2
18. 2
19. 2
20. 3
21. 2
22. 3
23. 4
24. 3
25. 4
26. 2
27. 1
28. 2
29. 2
30. 3
31. 4
32. 3
33. 1
34. 4
35. 4
36. 3
37. 1
38. 2
39. 3
40. 3
41. 2
42. 3
43. 4
44. 3
45. 3
46. 2
47. 1

48. 1
49. 2
50. 3

Chapter 8
MCQs on Pricing

1. Price is,

    1. Amount of money that you pay to buy a product

    2. Amount of money, goods or services that may offer to buy a product

    3. Amount of money you pay by cash to buy a product

    4. Amount of money that you pay through cash or credit card to buy a product

2. Among the four P's, the price is called,

    1. Most important "P"

    2. Most difficult "P" to get it right

    3. Revenue making "P"

    4. Most regulated "P" by the governments

3. As to price, what is untrue?

    1. Influences the buyer

    2. Prevents competitors capturing the market

    3. Most flexible "P" out of the four Ps

    4. Connects customers and sellers at the point of sales

4. Pricing objectives could be listed as:

  1. Financial, Marketing and Survival

  2. Profit maximization, blocking competition and Controlling the market

  3. Increasing cash flow, return on investment and market dominance

  4. Cost recovery, increasing market share and profit maximization

5. Three of the most important considerations in pricing are:

  1. Cost, durability and competitors

  2. Customers, competitors and importers

  3. Cost, legal aspects and advertising

  4. Cost, customers and competitors

6. If a company prices its products just enough to cover the cost and maintain its facilities, the pricing objective is,

  1. Financial

  2. Survival

  3. Loss reduction

  4. Cash flow

7. Pricing should be in line with,

  1. Positioning of the product

  2. Quality and Distribution of the product

  3. Promotion, physical evidence and processors of the

product

    4. All of the above

8. Customers are,

    1. Less sensitive to prices on products that they do not buy regularly and to the items that cost less

    2. Less sensitive to prices on products they regularly buy and items that cost a lot

    3. More sensitive to prices on products that they do not buy regularly and to the items that cost less

    4. More sensitive to prices on products that they do not buy regularly and to the items that cost a lot

9. If the percentage of increase in demand is more than the percentage of decrease in the price, then the demand is called,

    1. Elastic

    2. Inelastic

    3. Fluctuating

    4. None of the above

10. If the fixed cost is 100,000 and the Variable cost per unit is 25 and the selling price is 35. What would be the breakeven point?

    1. 20,000

    2. 10,000

    3. 4,000

4. 40,000

11. If the company's policy is to earn a profit of 50,000 per annum, how many units should be manufactured if the cost is 200,000 and variable cost is 40 and the selling price is 60?
   1. 10,000
   2. 20,000
   3. 12,500
   4. 25,000

12. What are pricing strategies used by Marketers?
   1. Fixed cost based and Variable cost based pricing
   2. Total cost based, Customer based and competitor based pricing
   3. World market and local market based pricing
   4. Fixed and flexible pricing

13. Market skimming pricing is suitable for a,
   1. Product that has so much of competition in the market
   2. Product that is innovative in high demand and low supply
   3. Product that is newly introduced to the market
   4. Product that has a short lifespan in the market

14. A product such as Rolex watches are sold at very high prices when compared to the other watches. What type of pricing strategy is it?

1. Market skimming
2. Market penetrating
3. Promotional pricing
4. Psychological pricing

15. A marketer is planning to introduce a toothpaste to compete with the currently available toothpaste in the market. What type of a pricing strategy the marketer should use?

1. Market penetrating pricing
2. Market skimming pricing
3. Psychological pricing
4. Value based pricing

16. If a marketer sets low prices for few popular products and assumes that the customer who enters the shop will buy other products too, what kind of pricing he is using?

1. Value based
2. Loss leader
3. Psychological
4. Tactical

17. A marketer is conducting a survey to find out what price the customers are willing to pay for a specific product that he going to offer to the market. What pricing strategy is he going to adopt?

1. Skimming

2. Penetration

3. Value based

4. Psychological

18. A Gas station owner says that the prices of the market are regulated and one company cannot increase the price on its own. However, he intends to provide a free windshield clean for all the customers who pumps gas from his station. What pricing strategy that he is using?

    1. Competitive

    2. Competitive advantage

    3. Standard price

    4. Value based pricing

19. If the cost of product is given as 30 and the company policy is to earn 20% on the sales price, what would be the sales price?

    1. 36

    2. 37.50

    3. 40

    4. 38

20. A marketer offers 20% off from its computer prices if anyone brings and return an old computer of any condition. This pricing is called,

    1. Discount pricing

    2. Promotional pricing

    3. Trade in pricing

4. Competitive pricing

21. In order to find the sales volume of breakeven point,
    1. Variable cost is subtracted from the sales price and then from that figure, the fixed cost is divided
    2. Fixed cost is subtracted from the sales price and then from that figure the variable cost is divided
    3. Fixed Cost plus the variable cost if divided by the sales price
    4. Sales price is divided by the variable cost

22. This type of cost increase with the increase in production:
    1. Fixed cost
    2. Marginal cost
    3. Variable cost
    4. Energy cost

23. The total cost is the aggregate of,
    1. Fixed cost and augmented cost
    2. Augmented cost and variable cost
    3. Fixed cost and variable cost
    4. Variable cost and marginal cost

24. If the price is marked at 100 to obtaining a 60% return on cost of the product, what is the cost of the product?
    1. 37.50

2. 62.50

3. 60

4. 40

25. Policy of Price flexibility means,

1. Permitting to charge variable prices for different customers.

2. Permitting salesman to grant discounts when customers bargain.

3. Adjust price according to the exchange fluctuation.

4. Permitting to bring down the price to the lowest in the market to win a price war.

26. Various marketers used different types of pricing objectives. They are:

1. Profitability, volume, meeting competition and prestige objectives

2. Internal and external objectives

3. Skimming and penetrative objectives

4. Psychological and Status quo objectives

27. A company like Walmart's lower prices on private label brands would fall onto:

1. Meeting competition objectives

2. Penetrating price objectives

3. Volume objectives

4. Social objectives

28. Analysis indicates that 10% increase in price will only reduce sales by 7% and 11% increase in sales price will reduce the sale by 12%. This analysis is important for,

    1. Target – return objectives

    2. Price impact evaluation

    3. Profit maximization objectives

    4. None of the above

29. Target- return pricing objectives,

    1. Are only long-term goals set to recover the investment

    2. Are only short-term goals set top recover the cost of the products sold

    3. Are focused on sales in a targeted market

    4. Short term or long-term pricing objectives of achieving a specified return on either sales or investment

30. Market share pricing objective,

    1. Is to dominate part of the market

    2. Is to capture portion of the market

    3. Is to share the market with other competitors

    4. Is to get a competitive advantage over the competitors

31. Price is a major factor in deciding to buy which of the following?

1. A cola drink
2. A hamburger
3. A mobile phone
4. Mobile service provider

32. If a pricing strategy emphasizes the benefits of its products in comparison to the price and quality of competitive products, it is,
    1. Value pricing
    2. Competitive pricing
    3. Target pricing
    4. Profit maximization pricing

33. Pricing objectives that are not related to either profitability or sales volume and quoting relatively very high prices are called,
    1. Return on investment
    2. Cash Flow
    3. Prestige
    4. Market leader

34. A non-profit organization organizing a dinner to raise funds for awareness program on dangers of rash driving, sets $500 per dinner plate. They are on a pricing objective of,
    1. Value pricing
    2. Social cause pricing

3. Profit maximization

4. Cost recovery

35. Pure completion is,

1. A market structure with few buyer and sellers that no single participant can influence the price.

2. A market structure with few buyer and many sellers that no participant can influence the price.

3. A market structure with many buyer and few sellers that top sellers can influence the price.

4. A market structure with many buyers and many sellers that no one can influence the price.

36. When a single seller controls the market and prices it is called,

1. Monopoly
2. Oligopoly
3. Monopolistic competition
4. None of the above

37. Oligopoly means,

1. Where few sellers compete
2. Start-up cost form barriers to keep out new competitors
3. Markets where oil is traded
4. Above 1 and 2 are correct

38. What is meant by "step out pricing practice"?

   1. A marketer fix a price and step out of the market

   2. A marketer raises the prices and then waits to see if others follow suit

   3. Stepping out of the market and wait and see how prices fluctuate

   4. Let your pricing behavior allow the competitors to know that you are going to step out of the market

39. What pricing strategy is suitable for new products offered by pharmaceutical companies who spend a, high cost on research and development?

   1. Value based pricing.

   2. Penetrative pricing.

   3. Competitive advantage pricing.

   4. Skimming pricing.

40. Marketers like Walmart and Canadian Tire compete with others by consistently offering low prices on a broad range of products. They are following

   1. Everyday low pricing (EDLP).

   2. Market penetration pricing.

   3. Customer perceived value pricing.

   4. None of the above

41. What would a low price generally create in the mindset of consumers?

1. Good image as a non-exploiter of consumer
2. A company that makes other competitors exit the market
3. Image of questionable quality
4. A company who keeps a very low profit margin

42. Payment to channel members for performing marketing functions are known as,

1. Trade Discounts
2. Functional Discounts
3. Quantity Discounts
4. Both 1 and 2 above

43. A marketer indicates that the traders would get a rebate of further 5% if the trader purchased at least 5000 pieces in a given period of time. This is,

1. Non-cumulative quantity discount
2. Cumulative quantity discount
3. Quantity Discount
4. Sales performance discount

44. A marketer informs its distributors in one of the regions that it will give an additional 5% discounts on the products they sell as they have an excess amount stocks in their stores. Once the stocks are reduced the offer will cease. This is,

1. Non-cumulative quantity discount

2. Cumulative quantity discount

3. Quantity Discount

4. Store specific discount

45. What is minimum advertised pricing (MAP)?

1. It is the tag price of an item

2. It is the listed price of an item

3. It is the agreed price by retailers not sell below

4. Prices that are found in advertisements

46. What is ex-works or ex- factory pricing?

1. All cost up to the point of delivery is included

2. Export packing, Shipping and insurance charges are not included

3. Exchange fluctuations could change the price quoted

4. Internal charges are included but not the external charges

47. What is FOB pricing?

1. Price does not include insurance charges

2. Price does not include shipping or insurance charges

3. Price does not include loading charges to the common carrier

4. Price does not include packaging chares

48. What is meant by C.I.F. price?

1. Price includes insurance and shipping charges

2. Price includes insurance, shipping and customs duty

3. Price does not include packaging charges

4. Price does not include internal transport charges

49. Promotional pricing is,

1. Prices of items marked in promotional materials

2. Prices offered at promotional events

3. Lower than normal price is offered as a temporary measure in the marketers marketing strategy to make sales

4. Prices marked as "Locked down" at supermarkets

50. What is meant by transfer pricing?

1. Price charged when an item is transferred from one shipper to another shipper

2. An internal transfer of an item from one profit center to another profit center

3. Additional price charged by a company when transferring a product to be shipped by a third party

4. Price charged by a company when transferring of raw materials from one factory to another.

51. Mark up price is called,

1. The maximum price that a retailer can sell a product

2. The range price that a retailer can mark the price

3. The amount that a retailer adds to the cost of a product

4. Increasing the prices of products that are demand and short in supply

52. Mark down/ locked down price is called,
    1. The minimum price that a retailer can sell a product
    2. The range price that a retailer can mark the price
    3. The amount that a retailer deducts from the cost of the price when the product is not moving
    4. The amount by which a retailer reduces the original selling price of a product

53. Availability of substitutes, classification of a product as luxury or necessary, percentage of the person's budget spent on an item and time perspectives will decide,
    1. Buyer behavior
    2. Elasticity of demand for a product
    3. Demand for a product in a given market
    4. Decision making of consumers in the marketplace

54. If a marketer experiences a drop in sales or a negative impact on one or several of its products due to a price cut in another product of the marketer, it could be called as,
1. Overall effect
2. Gains and losses
3. Cannibalization
4. Intra- competition

55. Which of the following statements regarding Price fixing and bid rigging is correct?

1. Price fixing is legal
2. Bid rigging is illegal
3. Both are legal in the competitive open markets
4. Both are illegal

Chapter 8
MCQs on Pricing

Answer Key
1. 2
2. 3
3. 2
4. 1
5. 4
6. 2
7. 4
8. 1
9. 1
10. 2
11. 3
12. 2
13. 2
14. 4
15. 1
16. 2
17. 3
18. 2
19. 2
20. 3
21. 1

22. 3
23. 3
24. 2
25. 1
26. 1
27. 1
28. 3
29. 4
30. 2
31. 4
32. 1
33. 3
34. 3
35. 4
36. 1
37. 4
38. 2
39. 4
40. 1
41. 3
42. 4
43. 2
44. 1
45. 3
46. 2
47. 2
48. 1
49. 3
50. 2
51. 3
52. 4
53. 1
54. 3
55. 4

Chapter 9
MCQs of Promotion

1. Mr. X says that he has a fine product marked with an affordable price and made available with all the distributors in the target market, but his sales are very low. The major reason for this could be,

    1. He has not packaged the product well

    2. He has not promoted the product

    3. He has not given discounts on the product

    4. He has not conducted a test market for the product

2. More comprehensive statement as to promotion is,

    1. Understanding the market and advertise the products

    2. Coordinating all promotional activities

    3. Informing, persuading and influencing the consumers purchase decision

    4. Conducting various promotional events

3. Mr. X works in a department where its function is coordinating all promotional activities: media advertising, direct mail, personal selling, sales promotions, public relations and sponsorships, to produce a unified customer-focused promotional message. He works at,

    1. Advertising Department

    2. Marketing Coordinating Department

    3. Agency Management Department

    4. Integrated Marketing Communication Department

4. Promotional mix could be identified as,

    1. Market research, advertising, sales promotion and direct marketing

    2. Advertising, Sales promotion, Publicity, Personal selling and Direct marketing

    3. Radio, Newspaper, Television, Internet, Poster and Banners

    4. Events, Publicity programs, exhibitions and sponsorships

5. There are three distinctive characteristics of advertising:

    1. Sound, movement and visibility

    2. Personal communication, expressiveness and clarity

    3. Public presentation, Amplified expressiveness and impersonality

    4. Audience grabbing, attraction and instance response

6. When a new product is introduced to the market, the advertising is commonly used to,

    1. Remind the consumers

    2. Persuade the consumers

    3. Motivate the consumers

    4. Inform the consumers

7. Mature products in the market such as Coca Cola uses advertising to,

    1. Remind the consumers

    2. Persuade the consumers

    3. Motivate the consumers

    4. Block new comers

8. One of the major advantage of radio when compared to television is,

    1. There are many radio channels than television channels

    2. Radio is always cheaper than the television

    3. One need not be sitting in front of radio to grasp the message

    4. Radios are portable

9. Effectiveness of radio is measured by,

    1. Reach and coverage

    2. Quality of the transmission

    3. Coverage

    4. Reach and listenership

10. Although radio, television and the social media have taken major part of advertising still………………………… play/plays a vital role.

    1. Press

    2. Hoardings

3. Sponsorships

4. Exhibitions

11. Public relations or Publicity has distinctive advantages over other tools of promotion. The reason for this is,

    1. High credibility, off guard and involves no media cost

    2. It could be used to relate important aspects outside the marketing realm

    3. Marketer has the control of publication of PR articles

    4. Both above 1 and 2 are correct

12. Personal selling is,

    1. Selling products for personal use

    2. Selling products to persons known to the seller

    3. Face to face interaction with customers for purpose of making a sale

    4. Helping customers to select products

13. One of the below does not belong to Direct Marketing:

    1. Mail by post and email

    2. SMS and MMS

    3. WhatsApp, Twitter or Viber message

    4. Door to door sales

14. Recently, there has been a notable increase in the promotional budgets in,

1. Social media marketing
2. Radio advertising
3. Television advertising
4. Press advertising

15. What is permission marketing?

1. Sending advertising messages to customers who have agreed in advance to receive commercial messages form the marketer.
2. Obtaining permission from companies to visit their business office and sell products to their staff.
3. Permitting marketing personnel to work from home and get orders.
4. Obtaining permission from a local authority to market products of the marketer at a festival taking place in the area belongs to the local authority.

16. What does product placement mean?

1. Displaying the product in a vantage point in a supermarket
2. Placing products in eye level racks in a supermarket
3. Paying a motion picture or television program producer to display a product in the film
4. Placing products as samples for the customers to test/taste in a wholesale or retail market

17. Using unconventional, innovative and low-cost techniques to attract consumers' attention is called,

  1. Out of the box marketing

  2. Novel advertising

  3. Disruptive marketing

  4. Guerrilla marketing

18. Buzz marketing or word-of-mouth marketing is used mainly by,

  1. Multinationals

  2. Marketers who do not have big budgets for mainstream advertising

  3. Marketers who sell fad items

  4. Marketers who like people to have an informal discussion about their products

19. A company uses a famous song with interesting animated video and places their products randomly in the video. They publish it on YouTube and shares it through Facebook. People also start sharing it as the video is entertaining and interesting. What is this called?

  1. It is Facebook marketing

  2. It is video marketing

  3. It is viral marketing

  4. It is internet marketing

20. Which of the following should not be conducted always as the effect of it will be lost?

  1. Advertising

  2. Sales promotion

3. Public relations
4. Personal selling

21. What are the first three steps in marketing communication planning?

1. Select the promo mix, select the communication channels and schedule promo activities
2. Schedule the promote activity, Sett the promo budgets and measure the results
3. Identify the target audience, Determine the communication objectives and develop communication strategy
4. Identify the target audience, Design the messages, schedule the promo activities

22. What is the importance of drawing a perceptual map for communication strategy?

1. It shows where your brand stands in comparison to other brands
2. It shows how competitors are fighting with each other
3. It shows overall company performance in the market
4. It shows crowded market place

23. Communication objectives should be SMART (Specific, measurable, achievable, realistic and time bound). What is the correct objective below as per the above criteria?

1. Create awareness of the brand among 25% of the

customers within the first six months

2. Create awareness of the brand within six months

3. Create awareness of the brand in the target market X within the first six months

4. Create awareness of the brand among 25% of the customers within the first six months in the target market X.

24. Communication objectives should have three basic elements:

1. It should make customers aware, provide incentives to buy and make them give a feedback.

2. It should influence the perception, attitudes and action of customers.

3. It should beat the competition, dominate the field of advertising and promote the brand

4. It should show the features and benefits of the product and the importance of buying it

25. In the Pull Strategy of communication, the promotional activities are mainly focused on,

1. Intermediaries
2. Customers
3. Low end of the market
4. High end of the market

26. In the Push Strategy of communication, the promotional

activities are mainly focused on,

1. Intermediaries
2. Customers
3. Low end of the market
4. High end of the market

27. In designing communication messages, different types of appeals are used. Few of the famous appeals are:

1. Economic appeal, social appeal and positive appeal
2. Rational appeal, positive appeal and emotional appeal
3. Benefit appeal, social appeal and economic appeal
4. Rational appeal, emotional appeal and moral appeal

28. If an advertisement shows a two-sided argument and concludes in drawing a positive outcome to a marketer's brand, it is a,

1. Moral appeal
2. Emotional appeal
3. economic appeal
4. Rational appeal

29. If an NGO shows a poor African child's desperate face in an appeal for donations to improve the economic development of that country, it is using a,

1. Moral appeal
2. Donation appeal
3. Emotional appeal

4. Economic appeal

30. One of the major elements that one should consider in selecting celebrity to appear in an advertisement is,

    1. How attractive the person is

    2. Can he or she be associated with the product

    3. How much he/she charges to appear in the advertisement

    4. Coming to an agreement that he or she should not appear in other advertisements

31. One of the below does not belong to Non- personal channels:

    1. TV and radio

    2. Newspaper and magazines

    3. email and standard post

    4. Hoarding and posters

32. Advertising can be divided in two broad categories:

    1. Conventional and non-conventional

    2. Standard and non-standard

    3. company managed and agency managed

    4. Above the Line (ATL), Below the Line (BTL)

33. Communication budget allocations are based on different methods. One of the below is not a widely used method:

    1. Objective or task method.

    2. Consumer demand method.

    3. Competitive parity method.

    4. Percentage on sales method.

34. **When communication mix is selected, order of importance for a consumer product communication mix would be:**

    1. Advertising, Sales promotion, Personal selling and Publicity.

    2. Personal selling, Sales promotion, Advertising and Public relations.

    3. Sales promotion, Public relations, Advertising and Personal Selling.

    4. Publicity, Advertising, Sales Promotion and Personal selling.

35. **What is it meant by the acronym AIDA in communication?**

    1. Attraction, Interest, Demand and Acceptance

    2. Attention, Interest, Desire and Action

    3. Acceptance, Integrity, Determined and Agility

    4. Always, Interest, Desire, Available

36. **It is always important to note level of target audience comprehension level in ……………….. a message.**

    1. Decoding

    2. Encoding

    3. Sending

    4. Receiving

37. **When an advertisement for example appears in the**

television, there could many distractions within the house and the viewer may not exactly grasp what the advertisement trying to portray. In communication jargon, this is called,

1. Environment in the house
2. Cognitive Dissonance
3. Noise
4. Disturbance

38. A company, who is not a sponsor a football game, sends a team comprised of its staff members to cheer for the match, with each one wearing a T-shirt with a letter of the brand name of the company. They stand together in cheering to show the brand name vividly. This planned activity could be interpreted as,

1. Ambush marketing
2. Team marketing
3. Sports marketing
4. Personal Marketing

39. Unprecedented level of increase in social media and internet based marketing has opened new avenues to,

1. Direct marketing
2. Personal selling
3. B to B marketing
4. Luxury goods marketing

40. Most of the countries have passed legislation to control Telemarketing as it has become annoying and a nuisance to

consumers. However, following are exempted in most of the countries,

    1. Survey research firms and Political parties

    2. Registered Charities and companies that already have a relationship with the customer.

    3. Both above and 1 and 2

    4. None of the above is correct

Chapter 9
MCQs of Promotion

Answers key

1. 2
2. 3
3. 4
4. 2
5. 3
6. 4
7. 1
8. 3
9. 4
10. 1
11. 4
12. 3
13. 4
14. 1
15. 1
16. 3
17. 2
18. 2
19. 3
20. 2

21. 3
22. 1
23. 4
24. 2
25. 2
26. 1
27. 4
28. 4
29. 3
30. 2
31. 3
32. 4
33. 2
34. 1
35. 2
36. 1
37. 3
38. 1
39. 1
40. 3

Chapter 10
MCQs on Distribution

1. Distribution involves everything that a marketer does in order for the customer to receive the product ………………….

    1. At the right place

    2. At the right time

    3. In the right condition

4. All of the above

2. Distribution strategy has two critical components:

1. Marketing channels and logistics and supply chain management
2. Supply chain management and Transportation
3. Storage and transportation
4. Packaging and shipping

3. Logistics means,

1. Controlling the various players involved in the distribution
2. Process of coordinating the flow of information, goods and services among the members of the marketing channel
3. Setting distribution tasks in the logical order
4. Tracking and managing the transportation of goods

4. Supply chain management is,

1. Controlling activities of purchasing, processing and delivery of raw materials
2. Management of suppliers and obtaining better prices
3. Coordinating the flow of information relating to suppliers
4. Developing a chain like link with suppliers

5. Physical distribution extends beyond transportation to,

1. Include control of activities relating to purchasing of raw materials

2. Include activities of developing relationship with suppliers and buyers

3. Include inventory control, material handling, protective packaging and order processing

4. Include managing marketing operations

6. A single producer usually manufactures limited variety of products but would like to sell in bulk. The consumer buys number of products in small quantities. This problem is known as,

1. Issue of buyer's and seller's choice
2. Issue of retail and wholesale market
3. Issue of Discrepancy of assortment
4. Issue of distribution

7. Channel function,

1. Reduces number of marketplace contacts necessary to make a sale
2. Standardizers exchange transactions by setting expectations for products and involves in the transfer process
3. Only above 1 is correct
4. Both above 1 and 2 are correct

8. Marketing intermediaries operate between manufacturer and

consumer. One of the below is not a marketing intermediary:

    1. Wholesaler

    2. Broker

    3. Stockiest

    4. Advertiser

9. Appointed Distributor of a marketer will,

    1. Handle all the distribution activities of the marketer

    2. Handles distribution of competitive products as well

    3. Use the name and technology of the marketer to manufacture and distribute

    4. Sell products to end users (consumers) only and not sell products to business customers

10. Stockiest,

    1. Sell products to end user

    2. Stock products and sells products through manufacturer's sales personnel and takes the responsibility of collecting the money

    3. Stock products in bulk and sell when products are in short supply to make huge profits

    4. Is a person who has very large warehouse facilities

11. Franchisee,

    1. Stocks company products and sell it to consumers (end user) only.

2. Stocks company products and sell to both customers and business users.

3. Use the name and technology of the principle on a royalty or license fee and manufacture or process products and sell it to all types of customers.

4. Stock products and pay the manufacturer only when the products are sold.

12. When a "Jobber" comes into play in between the wholesaler and the retailer, the channel goes to,

    1. Two levels of distributors

    2. Three levels of distributors

    3. Four levels of distributors

    4. Zero level of distributors

13. Direct Sales Channel is especially used in the past mainly for,

    1. Business to business marketing

    2. Business to consumer marketing

    3. Operations that require extensive demonstration in convincing the customers

    4. Both above 1 and 3

14. Optimum distribution intensity should ensure,

    1. Adequate market coverage for a product or service

    2. Reduction in distribution time

    3. Filling channels before competitors make their products

available

    4. Reduction in lead time in delivering goods

15. Intensive distribution is,

    1. Taking close care and supervision on all channels of distribution.

    2. Distributing products through all available channels.

    3. Intensifying distribution in highly competitive markets.

    4. Carefully selecting the best distributors in the marketplace.

16. Selective distribution is,

    1. Choosing only a limited number of distributors in one marketplace.

    2. Carefully selecting the best distributor in the marketplace.

    3. Selecting the distributor by going through the past performances.

    4. Selecting the distributor by image of the distributor

17. Exclusive distribution is,

    1. Giving distribution rights to the leading distributors in the marketplace.

    2. Giving distribution right only to one distributor in a specific region.

    3. Giving distributorship only to distributors who sell high end products.

    4. Giving distributorship to a distributor who will deal only

the marketers product.

18. Exclusive dealerships are usually granted for,

    1. High end branded consumer products

    2. Fast Moving Consumer Goods

    3. Non branded low priced products

    4. Government regulated products

19. Closed sales territory is,

    1. Market space in a closely regulated market

    2. Market that closes for customers periodically

    3. Geographical area that is assigned only to a specific distributor

    4. The shops within a big shopping mall

20. Horizontal conflict is,

    1. Disagreements among the channels members at different levels

    2. Disagreements among the channel members at the same level

    3. A conflict between the manufacturer and customers

    4. A conflict between manufacturer and distributor

21. Vertical conflict is,

    1. Disputes of channel members at different levels

    2. Disputes among the distributors at the same level

3. Disputes between regulatory authorities and distributors

4. Disputes between regulatory authorities and manufacturers

22. Grey goods are,

1. Products produced in one market meant to be sold in that market and then diverted to another market

2. Raw materials of grey color heavy metal

3. Products sold illegally

4. Products that are smuggled into the country without paying customs duty

23. A vertical marketing system (VMS) is,

1. Manufacturer acquiring other manufactures of the same type of products and controlling the marketplace

2. Manufacturer developing production facilities with increased efficiency

3. Integration or acquiring of various functions throughout the distribution system

4. Managing channel with integrated information management system

24. If a marketer develops its own raw material manufacturing unit and retail outlets,

1. It is an act of forward integration

2. It is an act of backward integration

3. It is both a forward and backward integration

4. It is in the business of monopolizing the market

25. When a single owner runs organizations at each stage of the marketing channel,
    1. It is called Administered Marketing System
    2. It is called Corporate Marketing System
    3. It is called Closely Controlled Marketing System
    4. It is called Exclusive Marketing System

26. Physical Distribution does not include,
    1. Customer Service and transportation
    2. Production and promotion
    3. Packaging and materials handling
    4. Order processing and warehousing

27. Assume that there are 5 manufacturers and 20 customers in a market. How many transactions would take place if there is no intermediary and how many transactions it would take place if there is an intermediary?
    1. 50 and 25
    2. 100 and 50
    3. 50 and 25
    4. 100 and 25

28. The power of mega supermarkets such as Walmart can reduce the levels of channel to,

1. Manufacturer- agent- retailer- customer
2. Manufacturer- customer
3. manufacturer- wholesaler- retailer- customer
4. Manufacturer- retailer- customer

29. Door to door marketing personnel falls into category of,
   1. Direct marketing channel
   2. Traditional marketing channel
   3. Personal marketing channel
   4. Low cost marketing channel

30. If a strong manufacturer like Unilever indicates that their soap will be given distribution only if other products of the company are purchased by the retailers, the company is trying to have a,
   1. Tying agreement
   2. Selective distribution
   3. Total package deal
   4. Conditional sale

31. Which of the following is NOT considered a type of reseller?
   1. Wholesaler
   2. Broker
   3. Manufacturer
   4. Sole distributor

32. When a marketer distributes its products through a channel structure that includes one or more resellers, this is known as ……………

      1. Indirect marketing
      2. Direct selling
      3. Multi- channel marketing
      4. Channel marketing

33. The ……….. refers to the various companies that are involved in moving a finished product from its manufacturer to the customer.

      1. Retailers
      2. Network chain
      3. Supply network
      4. Distribution network

34. For custom made products, ………………………….. to consumer or industrial user may be desirable.

      1. Diversified distribution channel
      2. Direct distribution channel
      3. Shorter distribution channel

4. Intensive distribution channel

35. What is the most suitable statement as to an E- marketing portal?

1. Another channel of distribution
2. Electronic system to meet customers
3. The only way to have a shop open for 24/7
4. Easy way to sell products and services

36. It is observed that in the age of internet, credit cards and e-commerce, people do not need to go to another place to buy a product. Therefore, distribution in the eyes of consumer could be called as,

1. Channel to buy goods
2. Convenience
3. Delivery of goods and service
4. Buying goods at the right time

37. A concept of retailing devised by Philip Kotler states that new types of retailers complete a full cycle: usually beginning as low-margin, low-price, low-status operations but later evolving into higher-priced, higher-service operations, eventually becoming like the conventional retailers they replaced. It is called,

1. Cycle of retailing
2. Wheel of retailing

3. Nature of retailing

4. Conventional wheel

38. A retailer bases its major decisions on two fundamental steps in the marketing strategy process:

1. Selecting target markets and developing retailing mix to satisfy its customers

2. Selecting the closest competitors to beat competition and winning customers

3. Attracting and diverting customers from competitors

4. Offering better prices whilst keeping the core services to satisfy customer

39. Retailers study all the elements of the market segmentation, but generally in the end, most retailers identify their target markets by certain,

1. Psychographics

2. Geographic

3. Demographics

4. Criteria that are unique to its objectives

40. Slotting allowance,

1. Is the packaging and shelving charges that retailers have to pay for their hard working shelf filers

2. Is the tax that the slot machine parlors have to pay to the government

3. Is the Non-refundable fees that the retailers charge from manufacturers to provide shelf space for their products

4. Is the fees that the retailers pay for designing shelves and isles for product display consultants

Chapter 10
MCQs on Distribution

Answer Key
1. 4
2. 1
3. 2
4. 1
5. 3
6. 3
7. 4
8. 4
9. 1
10. 2
11. 3
12. 2
13. 4
14. 1
15. 2
16. 1
17. 2
18. 1
19. 3
20. 2
21. 1
22. 3
23. 3

24. 3
25. 2
26. 2
27. 4
28. 4
29. 1
30. 1
31. 2
33. 4
34. 2
35. 1
36. 2
37. 2
38. 1
39. 3
40. 3

Chapter 11
MCQ'S on Marketing Planning

1. Strategic Plan is,

    1. A plan that guides and the implements the activities need to achieve a strategic plan

    2. A plan that develops to win competition with a strong competitor in the market place

3. Process of determining an organizations' main objectives and articulating the ways and means of achieving those objectives

4. An action that is taken by a company to achieve short term goals in the market place

2. Tactical plan is,

1. Tactics that a marker uses to win the long term objectives of the company

2. That guides the implementation of activities in the strategic plan of the company

3. Temporarily withdrawing from a specific market with an idea of returning later

4. Unethical practices adopted by a marketer to grab market share of the competitors

3. Who is responsible in strategic planning?

1. Marketing Director

2. Top Management, Board of Directors and CEO of companies

3. Middle managers

4. Marketing Consultants

4. In the process of marketing planning, formulating marketing strategy commences,

1. After mission, vision, objectives and business

environmental assessment

    2. Before all of the activities stated in answer number one

    3. Soon after the objectives

    4. After setting the sales objectives

5. A company is in the process of analyzing the strength of its major competitors. In what stage of the planning process is this activity done?

    1. In making organizational objectives

    2. In the stage of operational plans

    3. In the stage of business environmental assessment

    4. At the stage of monitoring activities

6. An objective to be effective, it should be SMART. What is meant by that?

    1. Sound, Meaningful, Articulate, Real and Time bound

    2. Serious, Marketable, Achievable, reasonable and tactful

    3. Specific, Measurable, Achievable, Actionable, Realistic and Time bound

    4. Superior, measurable, anticipatory, reachable and tested

7. Michael Porters Five Force model evaluates:

    1. Attractiveness and risk in the market for the firm

    2. Size of the market and its competitors

    3. Consumer buyer behavior

    4. Innovations taking place in marketing planning

8. If the bargaining power of buyers is high,

    1. It makes the firm strong in dealing with buyers

    2. It makes the firm weak in dealing with buyers

    3. It does not make any difference in dealing with buyers

    4. Buyers cannot dictate terms to the firm

9. The elements of SWOT analysis is,

    1. Strength, Work, Organization and Technology

    2. Sourcing, Worldwide, Open, Treaties

    3. Strength, Weaknesses, Opportunities Threats

    4. Sectional, Workings, Offences, Trust

10. Most of the sales forecasting methods bases historical data for future predictions. One of the below is not a method that bases historical data for forecasting:

    1. Weighted average

    2. Moving average

    3. Trend Analysis

    4. Market Survey- Market Test

11. A firm finds a best fit period that the core requirement of the market and particular competencies of the company fits together. It is called,

1. Target Market
2. Penetration point
3. Strategic window
4. Niche Market

12. In marketing terminology, the selected group of people that a company intends to serve through its goods and service is called,
1. Selected market
2. Mass market
3. Target market
4. Potential market

13. In the Boston Consulting Group's Market Share/Market Growth Matrix, Stars represent,
1. High market share in low growth markets
2. Low market share in low growth markets
3. High market share in low growth markets
4. High market share in high growth markets

14. In the Boston Consulting Group's Market Share/Market Growth Matrix, Question Marks represent,
1. Business units that generate little profit
2. Business units that have potential to become stars or cash cows
3. Business units that generate considerable income
4. Business units that generate strong cash flows

15. In the Boston Consulting Group's Market Share/Market Growth Matrix, if a business unit is a Cash Cow,

    1. It should consider withdrawing from the market

    2. It should use profits to finance growth of stars and question marks

    3. It should invest more fund for future growth

    4. It should either invest more funds for growth or consider divesting

16. In the Boston Consulting Group's Market Share/Market Growth Matrix, if the business unit is generating little profits, it is called,

    1. Dogs

    2. Stars

    3. Cash cow

    4. Question Marks

17. In the Boston Consulting Group's Market Share/Market Growth Matrix, "Question Marks" are included in the quadrant of,

    1. High industry growth but low relative market share

    2. High industry growth and high relative market share

    3. Low industry growth and low relative market share

    4. Low industry growth but high relative market share

18. In the Boston Consulting Group's Market Share/Market Growth Matrix, "Dogs" are included in the quadrant of,

1. High industry growth but low relative market share
2. High industry growth and high relative market share
3. Low industry growth and low relative market share
4. Low industry growth but high relative market share

19. Strategic Business Unit (SBU) in a business may have its own mangers, resources, objectives and competitors. It could be a,

1. Relatively autonomous division within a company
2. A product line of a division of a company
3. A single product of a product line of a company
4. Any of the above

20. To find out the market status of the different strategic business units, the most widely used method is,

1. Michael Porter's Five Force model
2. Boston Consulting Groups BCG Matrix
3. Ansof's Growth Opportunity Matrix
4. SWOT Analysis

21. In Ansof's Strategic Growth Opportunity Matrix, "Market Penetration" is,

1. Selling existing products in a new market

2. Selling existing products in the current market

3. Selling a new product in the current market

4. Selling a new product in the new a new market

22. If a company introduces a promotional program to sell its existing products in the current market, according to Ansof's Growth Matrix,

1. It is diversification
2. It is market development
3. it is product development
4. It is market penetration

23. If IBM manufactures a mobile phone and markets it, according to Ansof's growth matrix,

1. It is product development
2. It is diversification
3. It is market development
4. it is market penetration

24. If a local company enters into a foreign market to sell the same product that they are selling locally, according to Ansof's growth matrix, it is,

1. Market Development
2. Market Penetration
3. Market Diversification

4. Product development

25. According to Ansof's Growth Matrix, Market Diversification is,
   1. Entering a new market with a new product
   2. Introducing a new product to the existing market
   3. Introducing an existing product to a new market
   4. Promoting the existing product in the existing market

26. According to Ansof's Growth Matrix, Market Development is,
   1. Entering a new market with a new product
   2. Introducing a new product to the existing market
   3. Introducing an existing product to a new market
   4. Promoting the existing product in the existing market

27. According to Ansof's Growth Matrix, Product development is,
   1. Entering a new market with a new product
   2. Introducing a new product to the existing market
   3. Introducing an existing product to a new market
   4. Promoting the existing product in the existing market

28. According to Ansof's Growth Matrix, Market Penetration is,
   1. Entering a new market with a new product

2. Introducing a new product to the existing market

3. Introducing an existing product to a new market

4. Promoting the existing product in the existing market

29. Marketing planning has a .... process

   1. Linear

   2. Cyclic

   3. Multi-level

   4. None of the above

30. Marketing planning journey in logical order is,

   1. Where do we want to go, where are we now, how do we go there, how to ensure the arrival and Did we go there.

   2. Where are we now, where do we want to go, how do we go there, how to ensure the arrival and Did we go there.

   3. How do we go there, where are we now, how to ensure the arrival and Did we go there.

   4. How to ensure the arrival, where do we want to go, where are we now, how do we go there and Did we go there.

31. If a firm is analyzing Customer preferences, buyer behavior, needs and wants, decision making units and the process and their disposable income: what sate is the firm is in the marketing planning process?

1. Internal environment
2. Market analysis
3. Ansof's Matrix analysis
4. BCG Analysis

32. Once a proper SWOT Analysis is done, a firm should,
1. Consolidate strengths
2. Disregard the weaknesses
3. Only above one is correct
4. Both above 1 and 3 are correct

33. "Once the SWOT analysis is properly made, a firm should Exploit the opportunities and take steps to overcome the threats"
1. True
2. False

34. Company X is discussing about the what need of the market that they should serve, what are the sales volumes and share of market that they hope to obtain: They are in,
1. Setting marketing strategy
2. Setting marketing tactics
3. Setting marketing objectives
4. Setting Targets

35. Segmenting, Targeting and Positioning comes under,

1. Sales Strategy
2. Marketing Objectives
3. Marketing Tactics
4. Marketing Strategy

36. Ansof's Matrix is used to illustrate,
1. Marketing Environment
2. Market Status
3. Growth Strategies
4. Competitive Strategies

37. Michael Porter illustrates,
1. Market Growth Strategy
2. Market Penetration Strategy
3. Overall Competitive Strategy
4. Market Power Strategy

38. Michael Porter discusses three generic strategies in overall competitiveness:
1. Cost leadership, Production leadership and Market Power
2. Dominance over competitors, Blocking new entrants and Acquisition of substitute products manufacturers
3. Cost leadership, Differentiation and Collaborating with competitors
4. Cost Leadership, Differentiation and Focus

39. In the Michael Porters generic strategies, he subdivided the focus strategy to two parts:

    1. Competitor focus and Customer focus

    2. Product focus and sales focus

    3. Cost focus and Differentiation focus

    4. Quality focus and Price focus

40. In a marketing plan,

    1. Marketing Strategies describes how each marketing objective is achieved

    2. Marketing Strategies are more important than the marketing objectives

    3. Marketing objectives are descriptive and they do not set specific time lines

    4. Marketing Strategies are made after the budgets are prepared

41. Monitoring and evaluation is done,

    1. As an ongoing activity during the implementation of the marketing plan

    2. After the total implementation of the marketing plan

    3. Periodically after each quarter of the year

    4. By an external audit company

42. In an effective monitoring and evaluation system,

    1. It should not look into real time information

2. It should look into past records

3. It should do a post audit

4. It should take proactive action

43. A set of quantifiable measures that a marketer uses to compare actual performance with the set targets are called:

1. Performance evaluation

2. Key Performance Indicators (KPI)

3. SMART criteria

4. Bench Marking

44. KPIs do not,

1. Identify gaps in actual performance and set targets

2. Detect potential problems

3. Provide answers to issues

4. Involve in analyzing customer retention levels

45. Commonly most of the personnel in marketing operations perceive KPIs as,

1. Tool used to hold them responsible rather than motivate them

2. Waste of time in collecting data and analyzing rather than providing answers

3. A data collection endeavor

4. All of the above

46. Threats and Opportunities of a firm could be ascertained through the analysis of,
    1. Internal Environment
    2. External Environment
    3. Competitive Environment
    4. Regulatory Environment

47. Strengths and Weaknesses of a firm could be ascertained through the analysis of,
    1. Internal Environment
    2. External Environment
    3. Competitive Environment
    4. Regulatory Environment

48. In the ever changing market dynamics in the modern competitive markets, the short and long term planning periods are now,
    1. Decided on competitors planning periods
    2. Fixed as 1 year and 5 years
    3. Changed as 2 years and 6 years
    4. Periods are redefined to make both periods shorter than ever

49. Executive Summary of a marketing plan,
    1. Describes the details of the executives who formulated the

plan

    2. Describes the details of execution of the marketing plan

    3. Provides a brief overview of the entire plan

    4. Provides the targets of revenue and profits in detail to get the approval of the Board Directors of a firm

50. Although marketing planning is very important function, the critics of the traditional logical sequential decision making model argues that,

    1. It is a waste of time and energy

    2. Although plans are made they are not put into practice

    3. There is a need for flexibility, innovations and creativity

    4. Plans are part of the routine job and it is always adopting a top down approach

Chapter 11

MCQ'S on Marketing Planning

Answers key

1. 3
2. 2
3. 2
4. 1

5. 3
6. 3
7. 1
8. 2
9. 3
10. 4
11. 3
12. 3
13. 4
14. 2
15. 2
16. 1
17. 1
18. 3
19. 1
20. 2
21. 2
22. 4
23. 2
24. 1
25. 1
26. 3
27. 2
28. 4
29. 2
30. 2
31. 2
32. 3
33. 1
34. 3
35. 4
36. 3
37. 3
38. 4
39. 3
40. 1
41. 1
42. 4
43. 2

44. 3
45. 4
46. 2
47. 1
48. 4
49. 3
50. 3

Chapter 12

MCQs on Information and Communication Technology for Marketing

1. What does ICT stand for?

    1. Information and Communication Technology

    2. Internet Communication Tools

    3. International Computer Technology

    4. Integrated Communication Terminology

2. ICT elements could be described as,

    1. Processing data via computers and other electronic devices

    2. Telecommunications to connect people, process and distribute information, make sales and purchases

    3. Internet based social media and other channels, blogs and

other sites

    4. All of the above

3. "ICT has made a tremendous effect on marketing research, designing of products, manufacturing and testing products, communications, accounting and financial record keeping, tracking market information, logistics and inventory control."

    1. True

    2. False

4. ICT has become so widespread mainly because,

    1. It is easy to learn and install

    2. It is free or charged at low prices

    3. It is comparatively low cost and provides wider access to information across borders

    4. It is managed by an international body with widely accepted standards

5. A person comes to you and says that he wants to open a business that he could offer his products globally at any time of the day. He says that he only has a small capital. You would propose him to,

    1. Establish a business locally and appoint agents all over the world

    2. Establish a business and have an e-commerce site

    3. Establish a business and advertise all over the world

4. Establish a business and entrust the distribution of products to a multinational company

6. IT has made it possible for customers to directly access marketers and forward their specific requirements and order tailor-made products. As a result, ………………………. has been made possible.
    1. Mass marketing
    2. Niche marketing
    3. Focus marketing
    4. Mass customization

7. When a vast network of computers connected and exchange of information is taking place like a web, it is called,
    1. Extranet
    2. Intranet
    3. World Wide Web
    4. Google

8. A network of computers connecting communications throughout an organization. Different levels of passwords will give access to different kinds of information of the organization. This can be called as,
    1. Extranet
    2. Intranet
    3. World Wide Web

4. Close net

9. A network of computers connecting members of value/ supply chain. Can access producers of raw materials, suppliers of utilities, distributors etc. This can be called as,
   1. Extranet
   2. Intranet
   3. World Wide Web
   4. Distant net

10. Some of the companies started their business only through developing a website in the internet. They were not existing before in the physical form. These companies are called,
   1. "Pre Net" companies
   2. "Dot com" companies
   3. "Pure click" companies
   4. "Brick and Click" companies

11. Some of the companies had their businesses establishments physically before they started operating through internet. These businesses are called,
   1. "Post Net" companies
   2. "Dot com" companies
   3. Pure click companies
   4. "Brick and Click" companies

12. There has been a substantial increase in the internet based promotion and advertising during the past two decades as a result of,
    1. Comparatively low cost
    2. Increase in the use of internet and social media by people
    3. Decrease in the readership of conventional newspapers mainly with the younger generation
    4. All of the above

13. Which of the following is not a tool that is used through the internet for promotion:
    1. Advertising
    2. Direct Marketing
    3. Media releases
    4. Technical Support

14. Which of the following can be considered a potential barrier in spreading the internet usage in developing countries?
    1. Increase in the computer literacy
    2. Low cost of setting up
    3. Lack of electricity, fluctuations and thunder and lightning
    4. Government regulations

15. At the early stages of e-commerce, most popular products purchased through internet were,

1. Books, CDs, software, magazines, online films and information
2. Personal care products
3. Airline tickets and holiday packages
4. Unavailable products in the local markets

16. Internet based activities of marketing falls under,
1. Strategic Marketing
2. Marketing Operations
3. Modern Marketing
4. Interactive Marketing

17. A majority of the customers of products like mobile phones, go though the internet reviews and compare and contrast features, benefits and prices of competitive brands. As a result,
1. Personal selling has become very important
2. Substantial part of the decision of buying is made well before a person visits to a shop
3. Consumers get confused
4. Marketers have more power to convince customers through internet

18. Email marketing,
1. Is one of the most inexpensive modes of advertising
2. Can reach any part of world
3. Depends on a database of addresses

4. All of the above

19. The major issue in the fall in the popularity of using email for marketing is,
   1. Slow speeds
   2. Computer Viruses
   3. Regulation by governments
   4. Disinterest in people for the commercial emails

20. M- commerce is,
   1. Making transactions through major marketing portals
   2. Making transaction through desktop computers
   3. Making transactions though mobile devices
   4. Taking minimum risk in making transactions through mobile devices

21. Use of video, CD- ROM, Podcast, on line learning, e-books, online video conferencing etc. and the ever increasing road traffic and cost of transport has given a boost to,
   1. Residential college and university courses
   2. Non-conventional teaching systems
   3. Online learning courses
   4. Technology based courses

22. What is "Big data"?
   1. Extremely large data sets that may be analyzed

computationally to reveal patterns, trends, and associations, especially relating to human behavior and interactions

2. Big data sets that are used to predict complex behaviors like prediction of whether and financial markets

3. Data collected by big multinationals through various marketing research companies

4. Big data sets available for sale by google

23. Big Data has created issues as to,

    1. Computing power

    2. Limitation in the data analysis programs

    3. Matters relating to privacy

    4. Data storage systems

24. A unique feature in internet based websites and portals as against conventional form of marketing is,

    1. It allows marketers to make available unlimited amount of information to customers

    2. It allows not only the marketer as well as the customers to have a two- way communication

    3. It allows coupons and discount vouchers

    4. It provides links to other websites of competitive products

25. The customer expects quick response to their queries and complaints as a result of the nature of e-commerce and modern day nature of business. Therefore,

1. Marketers have to use super fast computers
2. Advanced computer programs should be installed
3. Trained staff with power to take decisions and follow up systems need to be developed
4. Websites should indicate that the time taken to respond

26. Many free utilities that you download from the Internet will install hidden software called ………………that sends details of the websites you visit and other information from your computer (which can include your email address) to advertisers so they can target you with popup ads and spam.

1. Malware
2. Viruses
3. Adware
3. Phishing

27. Combining Internet-based *distance learning* with face-to-face tuition is called,

1. Online learning
2. Blended learning
3. Modern learning
4. Interactive learning

28. The metric that calculates, by dividing the number of people who complete a particular action by the number of visitors to a particular webpage is called,

1. Conversion rate
2. Website traffic
3. Search engine maximization
4. Monitor shopping

29. The use of social networks and social interaction to encourage consumers to buy products and services online is called,

1. Facebook Marketing
2. Social Marketing/Commerce
3. Viral Marketing
2. Buzz Marketing

30. Software or applications that are hosted by a vendor and made available, on-demand through the cloud is called,

1. SaaS
2. Cloud computing
3. Open Commerce Software
4. Digital Vendor Facilitation

31. The online equivalent of a cash register connecting websites to credit card carriers so that online credit card transactions can be completed in real time is called,

1. Credit Card Link
2. Payment Gateway
3. Net Payment System

4. Electronic Teller in the Internet

32. Shopify is,

1. A SaaS (cloud) based ecommerce platform that makes commerce better for everyone
2. A shopping portal belongs to Facebook
3. Amazon's new portal for ecommerce
4. A High end e-commerce platform used by major e-commerce companies

33. The search bar is usually located in the top right hand corner of a website. It is usually the second most visited area of any website. It is called,

1. Contact us link
2. On site search
3. Chat link
4. Feedback link

34. E- commerce sites such as Amazon provide receiving, warehousing, packaging, and shipping orders of their merchant's products. This is called,

1. Order processing
2. Overall Solution
3. Fulfilment

4. Batch processing

35. Online retailers do not keep inventory, but orders received from customers and shipment details are transferred to either the manufacturer or a wholesaler, who ships the goods directly to the customer. This process is called,

1. Drop shipping
2. Hidden vendor
3. Net Shipping
4. Retail- Wholesale net collaboration

36. Best practices for web content producers to help boost rankings for keyword search terms in the organic listings of a search results page is called,

1. Website Advertising
2. Online Traffic Optimization
3. Search Engine maximization
4. Search engine manipulation

37. Search Engine Marketing (SEM) is,

1. Advertising the website in offline channels such as in newspapers and television
2. Marketing the site in the sales outlets and office premises of the marketer
3. Sponsored Internet marketing used to increase visibility of websites in Search Engines

4. Using internet based advertising agents to promote the web traffic

38. Internet marketing platform used for SEM on the Google search and display networks is called,
    1. Google promotion
    2. Google AdWords
    3. Google network maximization
    4. World Wide Web Optimization

39. A popular method for internet marketing where advertisers pay publishers for every click received on their ad, is called,
    1. CTR – Click Trough Rate
    2. CPC- Cost Per Click
    3. PPC- Pay Per Click
    4. PACC- Pay As Customer Click

40. When the actual cost per click is factored into how much the advertiser bids on specific keywords and the relevancy of the ad to the landing page destination, this is called,
    1. CTR – Click Trough Rate
    2. CPC- Cost Per Click
    3. PPC- Pay Per Click
    4. PACC- Pay As Customer Click

41. ………………………. is conducted by tracking the traffic coming to your website from other sites that promote your products and service, and rewarding them if their incoming traffic results in a sale.

    1. Affiliate Marketing
    2. Social Marketing
    3. Collaborative Marketing
    4. Third Party Marketing

42. Phishing is,

    1. The fraudulent practice of sending emails purporting to be from reputable companies in order to induce individuals to reveal personal information, such as passwords and credit card numbers.
    2. Sending viruses to computers and ask money to resolve the issue
    3. Sending messages about the famous sites to buy fishing gear
    4. Combing electronic and physically available sales outlets

43. A type of marketing that involves the creation and sharing of online material (such as videos, blogs, and social media posts) that does not explicitly promote a brand but is intended to

stimulate interest in its products or services:

1. Web sites
2. Web based advertising
3. Content marketing
4. Interactive marketing

44. A seminar conducted over the internet is called,

1. Net seminar
2. Web seminar
3. Webinar
4. Computer seminar

45. In the modern world of business, every company should have a,

1. Web site
2. Digital marketing strategy
3. Internet marketing division
4. Google Analytics

Chapter 12

MCQs on Information and Communication Technology for Marketing

Answers Key
1. 1
2. 4
3. 1
4. 3
5. 2
6. 4
7. 3
8. 2
9. 1
10. 3
11. 4
12. 4
13. 4
14. 3
15. 1
16. 2
17. 2
18. 4
19. 4
20. 3
21. 3
22. 1
23. 3
24. 2
25. 3
26. 3
27. 2
28. 1
29. 2
30. 1
31. 2
32. 1
33. 2
34. 3
35. 1
36. 3
37. 3
38. 2

39. 3
40. 2
41. 1
42. 1
43. 3
44. 3
45. 2

Thank you for buying this book and wish you all the best for your exams

www.ingramcontent.com/pod-product-compliance
Lightning Source LLC
Chambersburg PA
CBHW031620210526
45464CB00004B/1668